Praise for
The Youthful Art of Midlife Travel

"Chris Herrmann shows age is no barrier when it comes to travelling."
— Sam Okely, WIN TV News

"As baby boomers have begun rewriting the book on retirement, the idea of a gap year for later life has emerged....Two years ago Chris Herrmann packed up his life in Perth, Australia, bought a round-the-world ticket and headed off for 12 months....It was, he says, a fantastic experience – albeit one he'd never planned." — Philippa Fogarty, BBC Capital

"Chris' gap year not only changed his life but the lives of others — for the better." — Ken Wyatt, Federal Minister, Australian Government

"I wanted to thank you and let you know you have inspired me and influenced me. My kids are so proud of me and I know I have happy adventures ahead." — Jeni Walsh

"A brilliant detailed descriptive account of his travels. The historical events are beautifully told, about the people, places, events & occurrences."
— Wendy Howlet

"Amazing Aussie." — National TV Weekend Today Show

"Thank you for being an inspiration and giving me the courage to continue to follow my travel dreams alone, after losing my husband."
— Leonie Scott

"Absolutely loved it, lots of laughs on your wit." — Barbara Dunstan

"Loved the book, Chris is able to paint a very vivid picture and it almost feels like you are there." — Kay Svensson

"An excellent read and I felt as though I was also on the journey. Funny, witty, moving and above all, a great inspiration." — Christine Cormier

"Delightful and very enjoyable read." — Joe Pica

"Following your journey was exciting. To read the book was inspiring. A great example of getting on with life no matter what life throws at you." — Nicole Campbell

"Makes you want to get out of your comfort zone and see the world." — Rhonda Kremmer

The Youthful Art of Midlife Travel

One Man's Journey that will Inspire You to Live Your Travel Adventures

CHRIS HERRMANN

The Youthful Art of Midlife Travel
© Chris Herrmann 2019

All rights reserved. No part of this publication may be reproduced, stored in a retrieval system, or transmitted in any form or by any means, electronic, mechanical, photocopying, recording or otherwise, without the prior written permission of the author.

First published as My Senior Gap Year © Chris Herrmann 2018

Published by Shupaman Publishing
www.shupamanpublishing.com

Printed in the United States of America

ISBN: 978-0-6485222-0-1 (paperback)
        978-0-6485222-1-8 (eBook)

CONTENTS

Introduction vii

Chapter 1:   Life Is a Journey Not a Destination 1
Chapter 2:   The Outback. It's What Makes Australia Unique 9
Chapter 3:   A Marine Paradise 17
Chapter 4:   I Called Into Mars on My Way to Heaven 25
Chapter 5:   Getting There is Half the Fun 37
Chapter 6:   Spain. Quality Not Quantity 47
Chapter 7:   Hey, Let's Join the EU 61
Chapter 8:   Arabian Exile Experience 69
Chapter 9:   A Winter Wonderland 77
Chapter 10: Urban Swagging 83
Chapter 11: Central America. Plan B 87
Chapter 12: Let's Learn Spanish 95
Chapter 13: It's All About the Journey 101
Chapter 14: Travel – It's All About the People 107
Chapter 15: It's Dangerous. But I Went Anyway 115
Chapter 16: Terrorists. Really? 123
Chapter 17: Cuba. A Product of Two Extremes? 131
Chapter 18: Our Fascination with Old Stuff 135
Chapter 19: Each Day, A New Surprise 143
Chapter 20: Drugs. I Must Have Been Living Under a Rock 151
Chapter 21: Climate Change, Who Cares? 159
Chapter 22: A Dark Past. But There's Still Much to Smile About 165
Chapter 23: The Confessions of a Midlife Backpacker 173
Chapter 24: The Family Vacation. You Can't Beat 'Em 185
Chapter 25: In Search of Horse Cart 101 171
Chapter 26: What Now? 201

AUTHOR'S NOTE

Thank you for choosing *The Youthful Art of Midlife Travel*. This book was first published in Australia as *My Senior Gap Year*. A Gap Year is very popular with the younger generation in Australia and other countries. Typically taken between high school or university and regular employment, a Gap Year is most commonly spent backpacking overseas. A "Senior" Gap Year, particularly backpacking around the world in later midlife, has been not so common.

But no matter your travel preferences, *The Youthful Art of Midlife Travel* invites you on a journey where we step out of our comfort zones and challenge our fears and expectations of ourselves. More importantly, to travel with a spirit of youthfulness. Welcome to the youthful art of travel in midlife.

VIDEOS AND PHOTOS: Through this amazing journey around the world, we are treated to its many natural wonders and fascinating people. To help visually capture these experiences, multimedia icons are placed throughout the book. Scanning an icon with a mobile device using a QR code reader app will display either video or visual content on your device. For more details and recommended QR code reader apps, please visit www.youthfulmidlifetravel.com/thebook.

INTRODUCTION

I wanted this trip to be something completely different. To break away from normal routines. As such, no planning, no goals, no deadlines; just take each day of the next twelve months as it came. And that's what I did. Nothing more planned or booked than one around the world ticket, with three main stopovers, three to four months apart.

And I wanted to step outside the comfort zone. If it felt uncomfortable, I wanted to push myself to do it. It was the first time travelling solo and first time backpacking, certainly for any length of time. First time surfing, white water rafting, spear fishing and swimming in the middle of the ocean at night, being lit up with glowing plankton.

It may be the norm for young backpackers, but crawling up into the top bunk in a hostel mixed dormitory full of backpackers younger than my kids, was for me one of those stretching the comfort zone times. As with sleeping overnight stretched out on an airport lounge (thank you, Zurich Airport). And new experiences sleeping in a hammock and learning a new language (at least to an advanced kindergarten diploma level).

Homestays in non-English speaking homes, salsa classes while being coached by a sympathetic teacher and an interpreter; gate crashed a huge wedding-like family function…loved their whiskey; climbed up volcanoes; trekked up to five thousand metres and experienced the effects of high altitude; had my longest bike ride of over two hundred kilometres; swam with giant turtles and shared a park bench with a huge sea lion…I actually saw the seat first. Stranded on an island in the middle of the Pacific with not enough money to get off. And on another occasion discovered I was literally penniless in the middle of nowhere in a foreign country, no wallet, no money, no credit cards.

Slept in every conceivable form of bed from hostels, guest houses, dormitories, hotels, bamboo huts, homestays, on the floor, in a tent in the middle of a jungle, a hammock, a Buddhist monastery, in a swag and overnighted on buses. Stayed anywhere from one night to a couple weeks. If I didn't like a place I moved on. If I liked it, I stayed.

Travelled by just about every form of transport imaginable. From plush buses, buses with a full length bed, to buses with as good as no doors, crammed into chicken buses along with bums and armpits jammed in your face, squeezed into mini buses going from one side of a country to another, hung on for dear life on the back of a pickup taxi truck while peering down the edge of a mountain road.

Rode in a bone-shaking horse and cart; rode a camel; two days riding the rapids in the middle of a jungle; fished by helicopter; zipped around a countryside of ancient temples on an ebike… oh, and then had to push the thing home in the middle of the night because the battery went flat, sped along the highway on the back of a motor bike that looked like it was still being repaired, meanwhile fretting if my travel insurance was up to date, rode a push bike barefoot around city streets at night, no lights (well, everyone else was doing it).

: INTRODUCTION

Taken train trips that roll from side to side; you'd swear you're on an amusement park ride and in trains where you are constantly being flicked in the face by trees and sticks as the train carves its way through the jungle forest; taken a boat through the Amazon jungle and survived swimming in the middle of the Amazon without being taken out by piranhas or anacondas.

So let's go. I look forward to sharing this story with you. We've got places to see, stories to tell.

What's with this crazy idea of aimlessly backpacking around the world for a whole year?

Chapter 1

LIFE IS A JOURNEY NOT A DESTINATION

Ok. So, I was wrong. Those young people. Always taking off on a gap year. Why, they should be more responsible and go get a job like the rest of us. Turns out they are right. It's the rest of us who are missing out.

Sure, there are cruises. Floating luxury resorts catering to our every whim. Five star hotels for that well earned getaway from the hectic pace of life. But nothing beats rolling up your trousers, so to speak and going feet first into a different culture. Experiencing at street level the smells, the sites, the people, the food. Where your senses are stretched. Your normal standards of living and familiar surroundings that once offered familiar comfort, are stripped away. Being suddenly challenged with a new environment. And that's exactly what our younger generation are embracing. Typically well educated, or on the way. Hordes of them. In their thousands. Traversing the globe from one end to the other. And doing it with confidence, learning as they go. Engaging with local cultures. Exploring and experiencing different people and places from one country to another.

But I don't get it. Sure, us Boomers never had the opportunity to freely travel the globe like this generation. It seems as we grey up top, we lose our youthful ability to step outside our comfortable and familiar lifestyle. I know. I was challenged by the same resistance.

I must have dreamed up a hundred reasons why not to take on this adventure. The Mr Logic I'm here to protect you and keep you safe voice inside the head was working overtime. It was flat out feeding the head with sensible reasons not to do something that was outside the normal comfort zone. What? For twelve months? Travelling solo. Nah, you're too old. What if you got ill? Had a heart attack? No one would have a clue where you were. But why? You've got a comfortable life here in Australia. And then those middle of the night ones when Mr Logic I'm here to protect you wakes you up. "What if someone kidnaps you? It happens you know".

But something was different this time. For the first time in my life, the gut feeling kept coming through loud and clear. Whenever Mr Logic I need to protect you came up with yet another don't be so stupid reason, gut feeling would say, just shut up. Get over it. You're going. And that's what I did.

The intent of this trip was not a tick off sheet as to how many countries could be squeezed into a year. Rather, to establish a base in each of three continents. To be immersed in the local culture. To really experience it.

There was one other good reason for embarking on this latter stage midlife gap year adventure. The Government said so. The then Federal Assistant Health Minister, Ken Wyatt, had the same idea. He made an announcement saying when close to

CHAPTER 1: Life Is a Journey Not a Destination

retirement, we can all get burnt out in our jobs or business. Take a gap year he said and then contribute back to the workforce. If the government says it's a good idea, well it must be…right?

There was just one unresolved issue. Going for this length of time, I felt there needed to be a purpose rather than just travelling for the sake of it. Looking into a number of overseas volunteer organisations, it was intriguing to find most of them charge several thousand dollars. What the? For what? Apparently for administration and marketing costs their web sites quietly justify. Really? It wasn't for me. I couldn't come up with a purpose, but I was going anyway. One significant purpose would however, soon reveal itself.

This trip was about doing something completely different. To relive a more youthful and carefree approach. Breaking away from normal daily routines. As such no planning. No goals, no deadlines. Just work out each day of the next twelve months as it came. All that was booked was one around the world ticket… which cost only five hundred dollars. But that's another story. One stop in Spain. One in Central America. And one in South East Asia. That was the total extent of planning. Three stop offs about four months apart. There were a couple of short side trips. First two weeks visiting family in Austria. And a couple of weeks with friends over Christmas, New Year in New York and Canada. But the rest was taking each day as it came.

By now the furniture had been sold. The rest was in storage. I was about to shut the door for the last time. This had been our home here in Perth, Western Australia for the last five years. Perth is one of the most remote cities in the world. My wife and I had moved there from Adelaide, the nearest city, just under three thousand kilometres away. As empty nesters, we felt like a sea change. We dreamed up this idea of a Caravan Alternative. Most grey nomads invest in the big mobile rig – a four-wheel drive vehicle and large caravan. The typical route covers huge distances. Head north up through the centre of Australia, then south down the east coast to complete one half of the big loop. Then complete the other half of the country a couple of years later. This time return via the west coast.

The first stage of our Caravan Alternative plan was underway. The family home was packed up, except for a dozen boxes of personal household items. The boxes were trucked to Perth on the other side of the country. A tenant was ready to move in. A short-term rental in Perth would be our home for the next several months. Spend some time with family. Get involved in local activities, sports, etc, and use that as a base for exploring the local highlights. A low burnout form of travel while experiencing a new environment. Then repeat the same for the next three or so month stint at another destination.

It's not something you do overnight. There's a lot of disruption. Packing up the house, sorting what to take, where to go, organising a tenant. A lot of work, but, also very exciting. As a couple, we enjoyed working together on our new exciting adventure. One of the traps in life I believe, is the rut trap. Getting stuck in the same routine of life. Where the biggest excitement of the week is who's going to be eliminated on the latest reality TV show. It's curious how we get totally absorbed in other people's challenges and drama while we ourselves fall deeper into our own rut.

Some say, many people die at twenty five. They just have to wait another sixty years for their bodies to join them. Relationships

CHAPTER 1: Life Is a Journey Not a Destination

lose their spark. In some cases, the relationship dies as a result, often resulting in a huge life upheaval drama. So, my theory was, why not design your own drama on your own terms? That's what we did.

However, like all well intended plans, they often change. A few months in Perth turned into five years. We were living the family dream. Our kids were now establishing their own families. Grandkids were coming on thick and fast. Our children had been spread around the world and the country. Now by a set of coincidences, we were all living within a short drive of each other. In the same city. We'd regularly catch up. We could celebrate birthdays together. Babysit the grandkids as the family nest grew.

We had come from a large family home in Adelaide. By contrast, our home in Perth was an apartment. The views overlooking the Swan River towards the city centre were captivating. The breeze from across the river invigorating as it filled the home each day with a feeling of freshness. Perth would rightly rank as one of the most beautiful cities of the world. The view across the river to the city is exceptional. We took every advantage of our balcony's prime position. Many a balmy summer night would be enjoyed with a drink and meal on the balcony, often shared with family or friends. Working from home, a morning and afternoon tea on the balcony became a ritual. We used to joke with each other how we'd imagine people walking past would say to themselves, "Oh there's those two ol' farts on the balcony again."

Perth is also known as the city of lights. For good reason. A still night would turn the river into a huge canvas where the city lights would magically paint a spectacular reflection of brilliant vibrant colours deep across the river. This canvas landscape was forever changing. A gentle breeze shimmering across the river would add a subtle dappled glaze over the near perfect reflection. If nature was an artist, it was here at its best. The beauty was magical. We loved this home. The joy of sharing it with friends and family. Grandchildren running up to the door to be greeted with a special, welcoming, Nanna and Poppa hug.

But we weren't expecting what was about to happen.

Life was about to bring this special family chapter to an abrupt end. Many people had no idea my wife had lived with cancer for the last twelve years. Her focus was on living life to its fullness, not dwelling on it. She was always full of energy. We shared a common outlook of looking to the future. Not what if. But life now had other plans. Abruptly - within less than a week - after forty years of sharing the best part of our lives, it suddenly came to an end. We were still young. Just over sixty years.

Losing a life partner, a soul mate, had a huge impact. For one, it sharpens the awareness that you never know what card life will deal you.

It was now just over twelve months later. I wasn't hanging around waiting for my card. The rest of life could go on hold. At least for a year.

I looked across the now empty room. The walls bare of the family photos that once warmed our home with their smiles. The paintings that each told a story, now gone. The pre-dawn light was just starting to make its way across the river. A silhouette of the city spread across the balcony windows. I reflected on the many memorable times shared together, with family and with friends. The sadness. The tears. But just as much, the many times of joy and laughter we shared together. The songs we sang, the stories

CHAPTER 1: Life Is a Journey Not a Destination

and all the many good times that so generously filled those walls.

If we knew what life was going to serve us, we couldn't have planned this final chapter any better. These last five years of special family times will remain as one of our most treasured chapters.

I closed the door. Life is a journey, I reflected. Not a destination.

I pointed the car north and drove off.

THE PRE-TRIP

Chapter 2

THE OUTBACK. IT'S WHAT MAKES AUSTRALIA UNIQUE

This first six weeks was a six thousand kilometre road trip to visit my family. This took me from Perth in the south west of Australia through the Pilbara and the Kimberley regions in the remote northern part of Western Australia, and on to Darwin at the very top end of Australia. It was time with family. We went camping, fishing, spending time with the grandkids and even a spot of barramundi fishing by helicopter.

It's a big country. Up here you can travel all day, watch the sun rise, watch it set and you still haven't arrived at your destination. It's no wonder overnight pop up villages are scattered all along the endless highways of the outback. Populated from the thousands of caravanning Grey Nomads, it's a phenomenon that's almost reached plague proportions. During the day, long impassable chains of endless white objects crawl along the highways. The only respite for other travellers or truckies is between 4pm and sunrise. This is when the Nomads move into their temporary villages. Competition is fierce but outwardly cordial as these fifty foot or so rigs are jostled and manoeuvred to secure prime positions in the villages. Location, location, location is just as relevant here. Too late and you miss out on the prime real estate, lots of flat elevations and generous shade. Or worse still, risk missing the 5pm happy hour ritual.

As I rolled out my swag, I thought of my fellow Boomers as they enjoyed their nice soft beds and all the luxurious comforts of their home on wheels.

A visit to the popular Ningaloo Reef between Coral Bay and Exmouth, 1200km north of Perth had been a long awaited must do. The highlight was a scuba diving trip out of Exmouth with son, Travis. While the sandy moonscape-like seabed lacked any colourful coral, being "at one" with all the sea life is one of the very enjoyable pleasures of diving.

My biggest surprise was still to come. It was our second dive for the day. We were at ten metres depth. I could feel something on my back. But with the weightless effect I wasn't sure. Maybe it was a huge fish I hadn't noticed. Or perhaps something more sinister. I kept swimming, but it seemed still attached to my back. My worst fears had started to consume me.

I looked up to see what it was. And there attached to my back, was something I had not expected. Nor anything I had ever experienced on any previous dive. It was somewhat of a shock. Instead of some wild sea creature, I discovered my son sitting on top of me gyrating his hands up and down in an underwater version of, "Giddy up horsey!" We may both be adults…by age at least, but it's still these moments that make it precious to be a Dad.

People I met in my travels would often ask where in Australia they should visit. My view is a city is a city no matter what part of

CHAPTER 2: The Outback. It's What Makes Australia Unique

the world. But what makes Australia truly unique is the outback. It's a harsh country, but that's what makes it special. The vast rugged red landscape. Deep chasms. Rocky outcrops. Trees lined along the dry river beds patiently waiting for the next rain. And that can be years away. But when it does rain, it totally transforms the once strangled land, bringing with it new life and every colour nature has to offer. But that's just for a moment in time. Once that rain dries up it reverts to its harsh origins – until the next rain.

A place where in the long, distant, hazy horizon will slowly emerge an oasis. A respite from the unforgiving harshness of the sun's heat. A waterhole, as if totally out of place, lined with palm trees. Backdropped by towering red rocks. And with each nightfall, a gateway to the heavens of brilliant stars and galaxies emerges across the night sky. A place where you find the authentic, 'ow ya goin' mate' true blue Aussie Ocker character. They're as genuine and hospitable as you'll find anyone.

Like the Lyndhurst pub in outback South Australia. Some years back, after a day's travelling, we were hot, dusty and thirsty when we came across this isolated pub. There was little else around. But you didn't need any other attractions. The yarns from one of those outback characters were flowing as quick as the beers. It was one of those memorable trips you don't forget.

Alice Springs in the heart of Australia's outback. Trail biking through dry, rocky river beds. Climbing into Aboriginal ochre pits for a quick face paint. Swimming in an oasis surrounded by palm trees in the middle of a desert. Magnificent red chasms that provide relief from the blistering sun's heat. And further south, Uluru. That huge iconic rock stuck in the middle of the country.

Or our boys trip some years ago, taking a two thousand

kilometre short cut across Australia through the outback from South Australia to Queensland. Experiencing first hand just what the sudden transformation of this land is like. We were "back of Bourke" as they say. The unsealed road we were travelling was like a superhighway. That night we lay there in our swags around the campfire. In awe of the endless stars and galaxy above us. But as the clouds quietly moved in, what we didn't realise was those meaningless tiny spots of rain were about to change our trip. Awakening in the middle of the night surrounded in a sea of water. With daybreak, our highway the day before had become an impassable boggy track. Drenched. Bogged. Covered in mud. But what an adventurous, memorable experience. It's the nature of the Outback.

My next outback venture wasn't about to be as dramatic, yet was still another unique outback experience. If you could imagine a quaint little European village settled against snow-capped mountains, people meandering and pausing to chat along its little cobblestone roads that are lined with vibrant little shops. Strange as it may seem, but you could be excused for thinking that's what this small outback town could remind you of. It's not because of the rugged red mountains instead of snow backed mountains. Or snowflakes replaced with red dust that infiltrates everywhere. Nor any quaint cobblestone roads. Instead roads lined with grunty four-wheel drive machines, high vis clad workers and dozens of mums or off roster dads and their young kids that clearly outnumber the grey-haired members of a normal community.

It's probably one of Australia's best kept secrets. Tom Price. Home to about three thousand people. To the city suburbanite, Tom Price may seem like a last choice prize in a poor man's raffle.

CHAPTER 2: The Outback. It's What Makes Australia Unique

But ask the local cop being reluctantly posted elsewhere, who could feel for his child who cried because he didn't want to leave, or the mining electrician and his family who came here over ten years ago and has no desire to move on. Or observe all the energetic kids as they freely race around the parks and paths on their bikes, quickly pausing to greet each friend they encounter. The weekly BMX track competition that fills with kids of all ages, some barely old enough to ride a bike, let alone race.

Then there's Karijini National Park. Right on the town's doorstep with its spectacular gorges, waterfalls, swimming holes and camp grounds. It's that ruggedness that makes Tom Price unique. Where it's so hot in summer you could fry an egg on the road. And that touch of being unique. Where else would you have a road and a festival, named after the towns iconic Mountain that doesn't have a name. Mount Nameless. Seriously? Did they just forget to name that mountain? You'd think at least the local radio station would've run a competition by now to name the thing? But no, it's definitely no quaint little European village. But it certainly has that same community vibe, that friendly soul we all fantasize belongs in some cute little alpine village.

Tom Price is primarily an iron ore mining town. The town is controlled by mining giant Rio Tinto. But due to a recent downturn in the long running Western Australian resources boom, mining companies in the Pilbara region were cutting back. I had heard a rumour that excess bed linen from outlying mining camps was about to be dumped.

Sadly, we live in a ridiculously wasteful society. Have you ever tried to dispose of surplus furniture or household items? You can hardly give it away. Imagine if you had thousands of sheets, pillows and bed doonas to get rid of. It's probably no surprise then for giant mining companies, an easy way out is to just dump it. And that's exactly what I discovered they were doing. Truckloads of it being dumped at the local tip. It felt like a red rag to a bull. Everyone knew it was the wrong thing to do. From the employees at the tip, to workers at the mining camps. But no one was doing anything about it. There had to be people in need who could use this.

The question was who and where are they? There was one organisation that immediately came to mind. A decision made five years earlier to join this organisation, would prove to have a major impact on this trip.

I joined this organisation when we first moved to Perth. I was looking for an organisation where I could give back to the community. Their mottoes summed it up. Service above self and one profits most who serves best. The Mill Point Rotary Club in Perth. An active community focused organisation. I discovered an opportunity where I could contribute my skills and experience to a bigger cause working with other professional and motivated business people and professionals who also volunteer their time. Very much a social opportunity, but collectively working towards giving back to the community.

I was now 1,500 kilometres north of Perth. It was a Friday evening. Within an hour of sending an email, I had replies coming back faster than I had expected. Fellow members of the Mill Point Rotary Club back were listing off charities one after another who could use this linen.

The members back at the Mill Point Rotary Club were now making this happen. With the support of the local mining

CHAPTER 2: The Outback. It's What Makes Australia Unique

companies and some generous trucking companies, numerous people in need were about to benefit.

By the end of the project, an army of volunteers at the club distributed nearly 50,000 items of good quality bed linen. Provided to charities that support children and youth services, homeless, families in need, refugee centres, drug rehabilitation centres, the underprivileged, mentally impaired, as well as overseas hospitals and charities in developing countries.

What I didn't realise then was the impact this would have later in my travels.

 A city is a city. But it's the outback that makes Australia unique.

Chapter 3

A MARINE PARADISE

It all started fifty years ago. They built a railway line 300km long through some of the harshest land in the country. It connects the iron ore mine in Tom Price to the port at Dampier near Karratha. It's an impressive operation. Massive. In the middle of nowhere, huge, two hundred tonne trucks cart the ore gouged from these gigantic pits to the crushing plant. A constant stream of trains, each over 2km long, transport ore to the port 24 hours a day. I followed that 300km rail line from Tom Price along the dirt road to Karratha.

Son Nathan and his gang were working on a maintenance job just out of Tom Price. His brother Travis was working at the other end of the rail line just out of Karratha. I did what any good parent would do when calling in to see their kids. I baked a cake. A Beer Cake. It's an old family favourite. The size of a slab. This German strudel recipe dates back to well before my grandparent's time. It was always a favourite to feed the shearers. That's what I needed for this trip.

By contrast to one hundred years ago, these days there's a zero alcohol work policy. So, I went for a mid strength beer in the recipe. I figured it should keep them at least close to legal. They're not that hard done by though. A ute turns up. They start the generator. I gathered its only purpose was to boil the kettle. It was a short stop as they had a deadline to meet. I also had another two hundred kilometres to my next cake stop.

The boys love it out here. The biggest thing is the comradery. They're a good bunch of guys. I've met a number of them over the years. But it's quite clear to work up here you must have a name that ends in a vowel sound. There's Jusso, Cossie, Higgo, Little Higgo, Popey, Deano, Travvy, Marsee, Nayda, Hicksy, Coffa… the list goes on. If your name doesn't qualify, they tweak it to suit.

Dotted along the long stretch of train track are huge computer controlled, locomotive size machines. They go along the track, lift the rail and sleepers and then shake the daylights out of it before settling it firmly back into the ballast.

One of these Tamper machine locations was my next stop. After shaking my own way along this unsealed road, I found the turn-off for my next cake delivery stop. These machines are impressive. Inside it looks more like a plane cockpit with an array of knobs, lights and computer screens. But more importantly it includes a kettle. It was on with the high vis jacket and out with the cake. An interesting afternoon tea with the boys, with a difference.

The train line eventually makes its way to the port. Nearby is the city of Karratha. The centre of one of the longest mining booms in the country's history. Just a couple of years ago rents were astronomically high. Typically, three times what they are now. But with booms comes bust. And so do the stories of the highly paid "fly in fly out" (FIFO) workers. Suddenly finding themselves

CHAPTER 3: A Marine Paradise

out of work. Left with unexpected debt repaying the boy's toys of boats, jet skis, quad bikes, caravans and highly mortgaged houses. It's ironic the state government adopted the same boom time FIFO mentality. Now in debt because the royalties suddenly dried to a trickle.

So what they did was dream up this scheme to cut costs. Replace cops with cardboard cut outs. No, seriously. They're everywhere up there. Cardboard cops here. Cardboard cops there. Everywhere you look, cardboard cops. Outside shops. Inside shops. Fully uniformed gun toting laser gun armed cardboard cops. Brilliant idea. They'd be saving heaps, I reckon. Wouldn't surprise me they'd be looking at expanding this initiative. Not only replace more police, but have cardboard versions of nurses, teaches, or even social workers? The list could go on. But really, honestly, do they think they can fool us? I was chatting to one of these cops. It wouldn't have been more than twenty minutes before it became so obvious to me it was a fake. It refused to talk back to me. Dead giveaway. Come on, Government. You can fool some of the people some of the time. But you sure can't fool us all the time.

The boom may be well and truly over. But this city of around 16,000 people doesn't give the feeling its life is over - despite the cardboard cops. More so it would appear it's just the beginning. Mining production in the region hasn't stopped. Nor has the energy industry with major gas plants both exporting gas and piping it as far as 1600km south to supply the rest of the state.

As rents have plummeted back to more sustainable levels, once "fly in fly out" workers are now moving up here with their families. The orange flagged Toyota Prado mining vehicles that once defined the town are now drastically outnumbered by family vehicles.

The 'burbs have a distinct "I'm just renting" feeling to them though. In the newer residential developments, a quick count suggests a significant one in five or more homes are vacant. With job losses, breaking leases has become common as investors bear the financial brunt.

But regardless of all this, there's a definite community feel where young families enjoy the generous expanse of parks, walking paths, and an abundance of the region's camping, fishing and outdoor recreational opportunities.

In contrast to the city's 'burbs, is the more revitalized city centre. While the outside appearance of the shopping mall could do with a visit by Mr Westfield, the city centre has an emerging modern arty feel to it. Maybe it's the five dollar coffee prices. Or perhaps the trendy looking new low-rise apartment and commercial buildings starting to dominate the centre.

It's quite a contrast to the normal outbackish look. Yes, outback Karratha has now joined the city elites. Now complete with its own trendy arty buildings, along with all those odd bits of brightly coloured shapes stuck all over the building exterior, it is clearly a city in transition. My son and his family's decision to move here, along with many other families I met, is a smart one.

It's claimed they have the highest percentage of boat ownership per person of anywhere in the world up here. Not surprising. Karratha is at the door stop of a marine life mecca.

It's 4 am. The alarm sounds. We are off chasing mackerel out from nearby Dampier. As the sun rises, dotted across the coast line huge iron ore ships waiting to take the next piece of

CHAPTER 3: A Marine Paradise

Australia away are revealed. But the show stopper during the day was the spectacular whale show. From within metres of our boat to displays on the horizon, these monsters were flying out of the water.

The marine life is there for the picking. Fish varieties to suit everyone. Having said that, it's not that simple. It's not as though you can just duck out in the tinny, dip your hand in the water and pull out a fish for dinner. Having access to some local expertise is essential. That's where Deano, Trav's mate comes into it. The fishing master. Highly skilled and knowledgeable, yet patient and tolerant to assist those of us less competent at rigging lines and baiting, let alone selecting locations that bring results.

I'd have to admit, I was apprehensive about this latest fishing trip. Spear fishing. If I hadn't been asked to go, I know I wouldn't have pursued it, but I wasn't going to say no. My biggest concern were the Snappy Toms. While reports suggest an abundant shark population, I hadn't heard of any casualties so I figured it couldn't be that bad. Snagging my first fish did help distract any such fears.

But even guru Deano, was subtly shaken after he speared his final catch of the day. Finding himself encircled by several sizeable sharks. "Not a problem", says Ginge, Deano's mate. "Just hit 'em over the head with your spear gun. That'll get rid of them. Just a warning though", he says. "Don't shoot them with your spear gun otherwise you'll end up with a casualty… and it won't be the shark."!

But the real highlight of the day was the hospitality encountered on one of the islands of the archipelago. We'd reached our bag limit. All that was missing was a hot plate to cook one of our very palatable looking Coral Trouts for lunch. We must have looked like a boat load of shipwrecked seafarers as we made our way on to this remote beach. But it wasn't long before we were being treated to delicious grilled fish as part of some special island hospitality we met.

It's not just the boating the locals love up here. There's also some great camping spots close to the beach. Like Forty Mile beach. Less than an hour's drive south of Karratha. Time was against us. The pressure was on. Catch no fish, eat no dinner. We all agreed to our little challenge before we left on our overnight camping expedition. Having established camp, we set off over the sand dunes to the beach. With rods in hand along with two bush chooks (cans of emu brand beer), two preschool kids and a dog. According to the widely used Wikicamp app, this location rates as a popular bush camping spot. It certainly was the case for the predominantly grey nomad population. They were here in force, clearly escaping the colder southern parts of the country. A young German backpacker couple (on their overseas gap year) and ourselves were the minority.

Western Australia seems to have this extremely effective way of preserving fish stock. To us at least. This also happened on our earlier "catch no fish no eat" challenge trips. But no matter how dire the situation looked, we always managed to come through with the goods. I put this down to the influence of Trav's eternal fishing optimism. It prompted me to recall those times as a kid, when he'd come home from school so excited he actually got two words right in his spelling test!

In this test of survival, our results were similarly locked in with two fish. But no more. No matter how much perseverance that took us into the darkening night sky. However, Trav was still

CHAPTER 3: A Marine Paradise

just as excited as way back in the days of his first spelling tests. That saying, show me a child of seven and I'll tell you the man he'll be, certainly rings true here.

Now what better way to complement our grateful serving of fish for the second course? Yes, of course, that all time camping favourite, a can of Parsons rice cream and a can of peaches. A campfire, a swag under the stars and a few more bush chooks. Two little kids in their tent with no TV and no cartoon shows, who absolutely loved the whole experience. You can't beat the simple things of life. But more importantly, thankfully, we didn't have to touch our emergency backup can of baked beans!

From the red dust of the outback to the pristine ocean. And cardboard cops!

Chapter 4

I CALLED INTO MARS ON MY WAY TO HEAVEN

It was like a picture of planet Mars. I could see the similarity to the place I was now at. Rugged. Rocky. And what vegetation there was, it did not escape the thick layers of red dust that defined the landscape.

Port Hedland. The busiest port in the country. Ships are lined up for days waiting to get a berth at the wharf. It's a few hundred kilometres north from Rio Tinto's iron ore centre at Tom Price and its rail connected port at Dampier. Here is another huge operation. It's where the rest of the major iron ore players, BHP, Fortescue operate. And where Gina Rinehart has finally realised her father Lang Hancock's dream to build his own mining operation. Mind you, she hasn't done too bad collecting royalties from the other players in the meantime. Combined, it's another massive network with more huge, two kilometre plus, iron ore trains crisscrossing the country. Carting more of Australia to waiting countries via this mega port operation. Hence the odd bit of red dust layered all over the town.

True, in some cases the place may look like an uninhabitable scene from Mars. But being quick to judge can be shortsighted. I grew up in a place that to the outsider, looked like another planet. It was a railway siding town in the middle of what used to be called the Ninety Mile Desert, half way between Adelaide in South Australia and the Victorian border. To top it off, the Aboriginal meaning for the town is "barren woman." The town featured a grain silo along the rail siding, a station master, a cop and a pub. So it did qualify as a town - just.

My parents bought the run-down general store and turned it into quite a thriving business in its day. However, to the Melbourne cityite stopping only long enough to get a drink, "Oh", they'd gasp as they swiped away the flies in the soaring summer heat, "how could anyone possibly live here?" But what they didn't see was the community spirit, the friendships, the sense of belonging that was so strong within the town. I expect Australia's version of Mars is no different. I was just a superficial traveller passing through, who wasn't there long enough to feel the community spirit. Though I did experience a small piece of community caring. The proceeds from a not for profit seafarers tour, provides a service to bring the ships crews on and off to shore during their brief stay.

From Mars, Heaven was just another five hours up the road. I'd heard about this staircase to heaven in Broome. Turns out the staircase only gets you to the moon. But at least I was hoping it could give me a glimpse as to what's up there. Staircase or not, to the thousands of visitors that swell the town to three times its normal population in peak season, it would certainly feel like Heaven compared to the colder south.

Amongst numerous resort properties, our caravan camping

CHAPTER 4: I Called Into Mars on My Way to Heaven

park was one of many. Specially allocated streets in our park are temporary home to the great Southern Grey Nomad species. Each year they migrate from southern colder states, along well established migration routes, to this northern habitat. Here they nest, eat and drink for around four months a year. This pattern has been known to exist for at least the last 15 years, where the same group come together to socialise at the same time of year, same street, same allotment, each year.

Regardless of the length of stay, one thing about staying at a park like this, particularly sharing the camp kitchen, is the interesting diversity of people you meet. There's the Project Manager and his wife who are on an outback flying holiday. Tent in the back seat, they've been hopping their way around the outback from one airstrip to another taking in some of Australia's most spectacular scenery. Or the cop and his family who have taken their kids out of school for a few months, swapping classrooms for invaluable travel experiences. The park's temporary resident hairdresser, home schooling her daughter on their twelve-month travel adventure. Or just the hundreds of other Grey Nomads stopping over for various durations enjoying the heavenly warm climate or the endless white beaches.

I'm not going to mention our fishing competency while here. Suffice to say we would have been better off sitting in our camp chairs in the shade outside our tent, esky by our side, couple of bush chooks in hand, simply casting our fishing lines down the park street. Bait or not, it still wouldn't have made any difference. "You need a boat mate", was the best advice we could squeeze out of these old blokes cleaning their impressive sized catch. Unlike the majority of other sociable and up for a chat residents, this old blokes club was clearly guided by a highly secret handshake code policy of say nothing, give absolutely nothing away. And that's exactly what they did!

But there's more than fish to make heaven. It was time to take the staircase. It only appears at certain times of the year and our timing was perfect. But as it turned out, this natural highlight was just an illusion caused by the full moon rising over rippling water. I guess I'll still have to earn my way to the Pearly Gates after all.

But I wasn't disappointed heaven had to wait. I had been looking forward to this next stage of the trip for the last twelve months. Even though I had to travel thousands of kilometres to receive it. We were now on a mission to collect the winning prize of local radio station, Red FM's Father's Day competition. I was joining son Nathan, the winner of the prize. Our mission was taking us nine hundred kilometres by road on the top of Australia from Broome to Kununurra. There are two options. The four-wheel drive, Gibb River Road or the National One Great Northern Highway. The first, more adventurous option was tempting. But time was critical. We had a deadline to meet. The possibility of several flat tyres on this unsealed road, or the temptation to go off road into some of the attractive natural locations, didn't support our need to meet this commitment. The downside, the route we took, there's not a real lot to see. Except if you have Nathan's eyes.

In the middle of nowhere, as we were speeding along the highway, he spots an unusual item on the side of the road. A reluctant U turn by said driver, we discovered a bag full of valuable personal electronic items. Obviously, the bag fell out of someone's car or van. Ten years ago, what happened next would not have been possible.

CHAPTER 4: I Called Into Mars on My Way to Heaven

Here we are on the side of the highway. Just us, a hot sun and hundreds of flies. The nearest settlement miles away. Not a car in sight. But we actually found the owner of this lost bag of goods. I hadn't come across any grey nomad traveller in the outback who doesn't use the wikicamps app. The app has become the outback traveller's bible for sharing ideal camping spots. A message in one of the forums on the app, resulted in contact with a very grateful owner a few days later. It proves we live in a connected world, no matter how isolated or desolate we are.

It was on to Kununurra to collect the prize. Yes, Barramundi fishing by helicopter in Kununurra for father and son. To this day he never has told me what those twenty five words or less were that he wrote in his entry.

We had figured if we couldn't catch anything armed with a helicopter, then we might as well give up for good. Our high hopes however became increasingly subdued as time got closer. "The water isn't warm enough yet", we were told. "You're out of season mate", we were reminded.

It was a 4:30am rise for the early morning take off. Barra or no Barra, flying anywhere over this part of the country is a prize in itself. To experience the sunrise magically transforming the colour of the escarpments. As it switches on a deep rich red background glow. Overlayed with a sparse green patchwork of spinifex bushes, eucalyptus trees and the odd boab trees. It was an exciting start to the day.

A sizeable croc had taken up position on the river bank, the pilot's preferred spot. He angled the chopper away, taking us further upstream, passing smaller, less troublesome crocodiles. We took our positions on the bank. Not too close to the water

The Youthful Art of Midlife Travel

in case a croc made a guest appearance, we were advised. I can understand how you could easily get cross-eyed up here. You've got one eye on the fishing line. The other is constantly scanning for crocs.

Unfortunately, the first Barra we landed was considered not good enough for the dinner plate. "See the brownish skin? Too much of a muddy taste," our pilot explained as he slipped my prized 70cm plus catch back into the water. Mmm, I bemoaned having prematurely claimed the bragging rights to the catch of the day.

Back in the chopper, we manoeuvred off to another part of the river. These rivers are the dry season residual of a king tide that flushes this massive mud flat plain twice a year, bringing in fresh supplies of the coveted Barramundi.

Nathan landed the rest, finishing off with a 78cm much more silvery keeper. Nathan's fishing skills instantly shot up to respectable bragging rights territory. Our Barra took over the Esky that had kept our celebratory beers chilled for the flight back.

Join us in the helicopter while we look for the next barra fishing spot.

One of the striking features of the outback in this part of the country is its enormous vastness. Huge tracts of unproductive barren land. That is, until the Chinese came along. But clearly, Australia saw them coming. They actually paid us for this wasted land. Hectares and hectares of the stuff. Yep, for a whole bunch of this good for nothing land. What a deal. It gets even better though. All they're doing with it is growing weeds. I know. I had these weeds take over my backyard

CHAPTER 4: I Called Into Mars on My Way to Heaven

once. Grows like wildfire it does. You can't even eat it. All you get is seeds by the thousands. These seeds just make more of these weeds. Apparently, they reckon the Chinese back home love these seeds. Chia.

Then again, who's the smarter one here? Like with all that iron ore we're exporting. Surely Australia could create more value than just being a quarry? Why can't we produce the steel to sell?

Taking a more serious view on this Chia farm, when it comes to potential agricultural land, if we're not doing anything with it, why not let foreign investors make use of it? We visited the company behind this huge operation, the Kimberley Agricultural Investment company, twenty kilometres out of Kununurra. We were taken on a tour around this impressive project. Where there wasn't Chia as far as the eye could see, there were earthmoving machines either preparing dams or creating new vast areas of laser levelled fields to flood irrigate their expanding crops. The land is levelled to within a ten centimetre tolerance so the water drains off into channels that is then pumped into recycling dams.

Before leaving for China, the harvested Chia seeds do some extensive touring of the country. Which is nice. Containers of the seed are sent to the other side of Australia, down to Bordertown in South Australia. There it's graded, then sent back up to Port Adelaide in South Australia before shipping to China.

This agricultural development is part of the second stage of the West Australian Kimberley Region Ord Irrigation Scheme. The company's ultimate aim is to grow sugar. The bottom line is it is actually making productive use of the land, developing farming skills, creating local employment and inevitability, service business opportunities.

Meanwhile our prized Barra was enjoying a sleepover in the local ice works freezer. It was time to part company. And so was our fish. By that evening, with the help of the local butcher and his bandsaw, one half would be enjoyed by Nathan's family a thousand kilometres back on the West Australian coast. The other half, nearly as far again in the opposite direction with me and my other family members in Darwin, Northern Territory. Nice Barra. Great experience. Thanks son.

It had been 30 years since I was last here. Yet there's one thing I like about Darwin. It hasn't changed! Sure, the population has near doubled to over one hundred and thirty thousand. There are new roads. More houses. More industry. More businesses. More shops. More trees. I had to use Google maps on my mobile to find the place where we lived for three years. It was then, thirty years ago here in Darwin, I brought home the very first mobile phone. Remember those? It was the size of half a suitcase back then. I did think I was pretty cool. I'd drive up to the front gate, then call the home phone to get the kids to open the gate!

That was not the only cool thing we did up here. I bought a ride-on mower. Not that I really needed one. The lawns weren't really that big. But the really fun thing was driving the mower around the house towing the kids behind in the dinghy. Some would argue it was a mild case of going troppo. But the fun didn't stop there. We'd enter this little beast in the nearby annual Humpty Doo ride-on mower races. We weren't the fastest, but we did pretty good in the ride on mower egg and spoon races!

I'm not sure if they still have these races. But it's that sense you still feel about the place. The character of the place hasn't

CHAPTER 4: I Called Into Mars on My Way to Heaven

changed. Even Mindil Beach Markets, the iconic soul of Darwin, I reckon hasn't changed a bit.

And why should it change? Sure, the infrastructure of the city has developed. But why should the character, the soul of a city change? Cities are like people. We typically want it to be something it's not. Take Adelaide. It's always looked to its big sisters, Sydney and Melbourne and wanted to be like them. Why? It has its own unique soul; why change it? We were talking to Gayle and Pat at the markets who were on a trip up from Melbourne. I said how I love the vibe of the Melbourne city. Their immediate response was yes, but they don't have the bridge! Ah yes, the good ol' Sydney, Melbourne rivalry.

There's another unique feature of Darwin that hasn't changed. The question people always ask each other when they first meet. "Where you from and how long you been here"? So, it's still very much a transient town. Even to the born and bred locals they say you still don't get used to the seasonal heat and humidity build-up prior to the wet season. They're convinced it's getting hotter each year.

There's a cruel irony living here. You have just what you need in a tropical climate. Lots of water and beaches. There's one problem. You can't use it unless you risk being taken out by a crocodile. Or if you manage to escape them, there's still the risk of being stung by box jelly fish.

Yes, it does get uncomfortably hot and humid and all you can do is just look at the beaches. But it doesn't stop this part of the world attracting a growing number of people who seek a casual, easy going place to live. Perhaps there's good reason the locals describe the meaning of the Northern Territory (NT) as

Not Today. Not Tomorrow. Not Tuesday. Not Thursday. Maybe Friday. That says it all!

This last six weeks of my pre-overseas road trip up the north-west coast of Australia was special. Experiencing it is to experience one of Australia's highlights. Its vast distances without an over population of people or tourists have in many ways preserved much of its natural beauty. For me, as much a part of the beauty this land offered, was the opportunity to experience this time with family.

I was recently inspired by a presentation by Dr Bruce Robinson, author of Fathering from the Fast Lane. The crux of the message was how to be an effective father against the fast pace of life and the demands of a career. There was one message that stuck with me. The significance of spending one on one time with each of your children. I remember the impact as a child.

The message was a bit late for me and my children. But the opportunity over these past few weeks, even with my adult children, was still very special. Along with all the smiley, laughing, cute, joyful, adorable, embracing and beautiful, loving faces of the land of the little people. You forget the patience required to live in this world. The negotiating that starts with the first pitter-patter of little feet down the passage before the sun has even had a chance to rise. From stars earned to stay in bed all night, to kamikaze dive bombing the morning cereal into a briefly cooperating mouth, to the last hastily concocted deals negotiating the final bedtime ritual.

Having forgotten from all those years ago, you can't help but admire the relentless patience demanded of parents. But unquestionably, these are some of the best years of life; sharing the joys of

CHAPTER 4: I Called Into Mars on My Way to Heaven

our young people as they learn and grow. It was a delight to share a part of this with my children, their spouses and their families over this time.

But now, it was time for the real adventure to begin.

More of what makes Australia unique while searching for the staircase to Heaven.

Chapter 5

GETTING THERE IS HALF THE FUN

We exchanged polite pleasantries as we settled in for the twelve hour flight ahead. We are by nature a territorial creature. Defining our space and our rights to it are as ancient as human existence. From children's play areas, to neighbourhood fences, through to national borders, we defend the entitlement of our "space". From peaceful coexistence, the threat of border skirmishes to outright war is ever present.

A simple armrest defined the boundary between our seats. However, it was clear before we even took off, our border was on the verge of disputed territory. I feared a silent conflict was emerging.

I don't know who designs these things. But how simple would it be to make these arm rests just slightly wider to accommodate two arms. And what about including a little plastic fence along the middle of the arm rest to clearly define the border and prevent any spill over into disputed territory.

No. Instead, hours of otherwise relaxing reading time are consumed with plotting the next move. Carefully timed strategic moves to secure the next prominent stake on this highly valued armchair real estate. This of course, also impacts drinking and eating tasks. Such activities now need to be relegated solely to the other arm to avoid losing the well fought out stakeholder position.

The only other option to secure any rightful share of this armrest border territory requires much more patience. Taking a position at the far rear end of the armrest. Any lapse by the defending party provides an immediate opportunity for the other party to advance up to stake a more prominent position.

As with any dispute, the rational and common sense approach would of course, be to throw down arms and negotiate a settlement. I thought about that. But seriously, how would you open the discussion? Would you propose a rotating schedule timetable, or split the flight time between front and back half?

I was fortunate. While we both had silently set about claiming our territorial right to this insignificant piece of plastic, it was clear we both had a reasonable sense of fairness. I didn't keep count. But I think we gave each other fair turns, without the need to uncomfortably raise the subject. Despite this potentially turning into a full-blown armchair war zone, we departed amicably, briefly chatting and wishing each other pleasant travels.

Perhaps in the near future there may not be a need to address the issue of potential armrest territorial skirmishes. There's been a new development in passenger services. It may just cause sufficient distraction. It's a new dating app for flying. It functions like Tinder but in the sky, connecting passengers for in-flight flirting and possible mile-high hook ups. In the meantime, if the worst of travel is haggling over an armrest, it's a small price to pay. Especially when you are about to step into God's Garden…

CHAPTER 5: Getting There is Half the Fun

That's right here, in Austria. In a small rural community, surrounded by snow-capped mountains. It looks more like a small village with its loose collection of houses rather than a farming region. The houses are large. They need to be. I first learnt this some years ago when skiing in neighbouring Switzerland. We were making our way through the snow back to our chalet. I'd never heard a baa sound coming from a house before. Here, near the village of Egg, it's not so much sheep that farmers share their house with, but cows. Most of the house area is a barn. A necessity for sheltering the cows and storing the hay and farm equipment during the snow filled winter. A practice that goes back as old as some of the homes. Some, as the one of my host, up to 400 years old.

The weather is now just starting to turn. The wood piles in each house are completely stacked up in preparation for the deep winter months ahead. Traffic connecting the villages is disrupted as farmers lead their cattle down from the mountains along the village roads. A long-held tradition that surpasses any modern day rights of vehicles.

It's an amazing transformation. From rich green fields to what in a couple months will be blanketed with snow. It's hard to imagine. The days are a pleasant balmy mid-twenties centigrade. An evening walk brings a mix of the sound of children playing against a symphony of chiming cowbells.

It's a picture perfect setting. By day, the valley dotted with clusters of houses, flowers draping over their balconies, the fresh green fields and the mountainous background, provides a scene fitting of a movie. By night the lights from the scattering of houses dimly sparkle across the valley up against the towering mountain ranges.

Apart from the seasonally dormant ski lifts, the only signs of tourism here are the hiking guide signs. The occasional hikers seen are mostly from neighbouring Germany. You get a sense it's a sibling-like love-hate relationship. Much the same as our Kiwi friends. When the chips are down we're there for each other, but in the meantime we're the butt of each other's jokes.

I asked my host if yodelling was still a part of the culture. Coming from German ancestry, it was a talent my father would display on rare occasions. It was the very likes of these mountains, as my host explained, where yodelling from mountain to mountain was used as a way of communicating. You get the feeling a lot of tradition remains very much part of the local culture. However, as with my father, yodelling it seems, is a past culture that's as good as lost in these mountains.

I was preparing a meal for my Austrian hosts in their 350 year old hut. It took a couple of attempts to get the fire going as each piece of kindling wood was delicately placed inside the small fire hatch. It was how I remember the way my grandmother used to cook. Old Grandma Selma could churn out her famous Christmas feasts on her wood stove just about with her eyes closed. This was my first experience cooking a meal on one of these bygone relics.

Perched on the side of a hill, the hut is about as original as it gets. Complete with stable, it had no running water except for a water trough carved out of a tree trunk. The trough is fed by water from a spring. Ancient wooden doors lead into a small kitchen and a dining room. A set of poky steps lead to a small upstairs bedroom. A large part of the side of the hut hinges down to create a ramp to the loft, providing access to store hay for the winter.

The well had only the day before been recommissioned.

CHAPTER 5: Getting There is Half the Fun

Apparently, it's not as simple as whacking a hole in the ground. I was told the timing of the moon is critical in locating the position of a well. As explained to me, as the moon affects the tides, it also does with the level of underground spring water.

The hut had only recently been restored to a stage where it's just liveable. That is, except for a toilet, shower, kitchen sink or running water. It does however, have recently connected power. This adds a touch of irony with a coffee machine and electric kettle sitting on the old weathered kitchen bench below the small antique styled shuttered window.

The portable hot plates I must admit were a saviour. With a huge pot of vegetables waiting to cook, it soon became clear that Grandma would have prepared her meal hours before I had thought of it. The stove at least provided the final nostalgic touch to keep the pot of waiting meal warm. And what better way to compliment this little cook up than with a few shots of schnapps, beer, wine and a sing-along to finish the night off. A lovely nostalgic night to remember.

But it's a weird thing. We strive to live in our version of a McMansion with all the latest mod cons. Yet we romanticise about a getaway in the likes of some ancient rustic hut. Or we'll relish the experience of spending weeks on end cooped up in a caravan that's not much wider than your hallway at home. Or despite all the comforts of home we'll go living in the closest thing to a cave, such as camping in a tent.

Whatever this quirk of human nature, an evening in this fantastic old hut was an absolute highlight. Let alone what it would be like in winter. Located near the base of a nearby ski run, there would be skiing down the slopes to the hut to enjoy a quick round of Schnapps. Watching through those tiny little shutter windows, the snowflakes gently falling outside, while that pot of stew is warmed by the quaint, old wood stove.

Apart from all these beautiful mountain settings, Europe has another side. I was pleasantly surprised to discover I was on the doorstep to one of Europe's most popular bicycle routes. More than that, a flat route. It was a must do.

Of all outdoor activities, cycling would be my favourite. Back home, National Ride to Work Day was always a special day. Not that I had far to go to work. But being National Ride to Work Day I'd still put on all my gear, the lycra, clip on shoes, the helmet, etc. Off I'd go. I'd start from the kitchen. And before I knew it, within seconds, I was at the office. What a fantastic and energising way to start the day, I would think to myself. Even if you do work from home.

Usually on the weekend I'd take Bike, as I affectionately called it, out to play with other bikes. We'd then all go riding together. I suppose it's much the same as what dog owners do when they meet in a park. Instead, us bike owners talk about how light our carbon fibre bikes are and how much faster we now go since we've upgraded to outer bearing hubs.

Bike is not as flash as some of Bike's friends. But that doesn't worry me. We've been through so much together. First thing in the morning, off we'd go. Really helps to clear the head, I reckon. Bike loved it too. Bike so loved seeing the dust specs blow off his handlebars. And I just like the feeling of getting the blood pumping. And you should see the look on Bike as his bearings warm up. It's so good. I remember one Friday evening, not that long after life had dealt a bit of a blow. I was starting to feel a bit

CHAPTER 5: Getting There is Half the Fun

woe is me, why me, that sort of feeling. So, I hopped on Bike and we rode the fifteen kilometres around the river. As fast as Bike would let me push his peddles. Interestingly, I had read one of the reasons why there's an increase in depression is because we are not as active as our forebears. Maybe there's something in that, because I came back from that ride feeling I was ready to take on anything!

The ride I was about to do in Europe was a bit longer than fifteen kilometres. It goes around the entire edge of Lake Bodensee. I'd only left Bregenz at midday but by the end of the afternoon I had cycled from Austria, through Switzerland and ended up in Germany. And that was just day one. Only in Europe.

The two hundred kilometre plus path winds through delightful medieval towns, romantic villages, sleepy-looking towns and through expanses of vineyards and orchards. Mostly on bike paths, the ride takes in spectacular landscape alongside the lake against a backdrop of the Alps. You could take on the challenge in a day. But let's be sensible here. While I did it over three days, most people would stretch it over a few extra days. And why not? With a group of friends…cycle for a few hours, find a nice quaint stopover. Then enjoy the rest of the day relaxing with a wine or a few. Then simply repeat the next day…

Despite the very flat nature of the ride, electric ebikes are very popular to accommodate various fitness levels. Tour companies provide pre-paid packages. But with the well signed path it's easy to do it as a self-guided tour. While it would be helpful, you can do it as I did, without a map and the occasional use of an online map. With many places to stop for the night, online booking sites add to the flexibility of finding accommodation along the way.

Riding through the little villages, I first thought, wow there's a lot doing this tour. But while the ride is extremely popular, most of these cyclists are locals. Where as in Oz, we'd rather take the car to the local supermarket. Here they take their bike.

I saw a recent documentary where they found the most liveable cities are where car usage is minimal while walking and riding encouraged. Less incidence of asthma from car pollution, and reduced obesity from more activity. Makes sense.

The majority of riders around the lake were mainly in the more mature age bracket. Riders vary from groups to typically couples or solo riders. I had the pleasure of teaming up with an Austrian I met along the way. Having a local like Herbert not only provided enjoyable company, but the benefit of a lot of local knowledge and translation assistance.

The most challenging part was actually after the lake ride. Cycling the twenty five kilometres back home over the mountain to the village of Egg. The bier at the local tavern made it all worthwhile though!

A fantastic way to see and experience a taste of Europe.... both the mountains and the flat. It was a fun start to the overseas journey. But the real adventure was now only about to begin.

From an ancient hut in the Austrian alps to cycling around a European lake through medieval like villages.

Chapter 6

SPAIN. QUALITY NOT QUANTITY

One of the criteria of my trip was to step outside the comfort zone. If it felt uncomfortable, then I wanted to step out and do it. That started on day one of my solo travelling at Zurich airport. I arrived by train late that evening. The flight to Spain was the next morning. It seemed too much of a hassle to find a hotel. I'd never slept overnight in an airport before. I could sense the discomfort. Not the bed. But, being honest with myself, more the "what would others think". It's a strange expectation we can place on ourselves. I mean, you wouldn't see some corporate manager or business person doing this. So, yes, I admit, this felt uncomfortable. If this was someone in their youth sprawled out on a couch for the night, it would look like, wow, they are on an adventure. Another not so young person would look like a down and out.

But I thought, I'm on an adventure too, right? So, I decided to do what any other youthful minded backpacker would do. Made a bed on a row of seats in the airport. By this stage the airport was in complete darkness. Lights out. Closed for the night. The only light was from the torch of a security guy walking around in the distance. You can't control other's perceptions. I chose not to think about it as I shut my eyes for the night.

The digital display was reading 300km per hour. Spain's fast train network is impressive. On arriving in Madrid, I decided to make Valencia, on Spain's east coast, home for the next three months. This was the first stage of the year long journey.

The contrast couldn't be greater. Austria, God's garden with its lush green rolling hills backdropped by majestic mountains. But now I was in more familiar territory to home. A landscape browned by the summer heat. The sparse number of trees now only sparingly providing touches of green on the endless, flat, dry landscape.

If staying in a four hundred year old home took me back in time, I was now entering a city that was going back even further, to over two thousand years ago. Valencia, now home to around 2 million people, was founded as a Roman colony in 138 BC. But I don't get it. I booked my accommodation using a mobile phone app while hurtling across the country at high speed. I then used Google maps to navigate me to the place I booked. But how did the Romans do it? Assuming they would've picked the first available seat on a chariot heading east, how would they've worked out where to stay? How would they know how people rated it or how it compared to others? And then to find the place. This place is like a maze. A complex web of all these little alleys and streets darting off in all directions.

I didn't know a word of Spanish. I was now completely on my own. I used a guest house for the next few days to find a rental apartment. I could sense the initial feeling of excitement being tested. The first place viewed, the only thing missing I reckon

CHAPTER 6: Spain. Quality Not Quantity

was the crime scene tape. The next looked more like a settlement area for refugees. Another, yes it was close to the beach, but the unwelcoming flat ten flights of stairs up was not something you'd look forward to coming home to.

At one stage my brother said to me over the phone, this is not working out too good for you eh? I did explain to him, it was not like one of these trips where you get to the airport to be greeted by a "Hello and welcome, Mr Herrmann". Then ushered to a waiting car and whisked away to your resort, where a welcoming basket of flowers and a bottle of champagne awaits you. No, this was all part of the around the world challenge. But I could feel that sinking feeling, "Oh no, what have I done" setting in.

I had experienced this sinking feeling many times before. Where the excitement of an adventure is suddenly challenged by reality. Once, when our youngest of three children was just three weeks old. We had packed up our house and moved from one end of southern Australia to Darwin in the top end. I can remember walking across the tarmac on arrival. It was hot and humid. Raining. With three kids in tow, it was one of our "Oh no, what have we done" moments. We would often think back and ask ourselves, what were we thinking. But that was the first of one of our best family times. One of the highlights of our life.

There were many more. Like a two year stint in Saudi Arabia. I can still see our young children, the youngest just three, heading off in the school bus in the middle of Riyadh. Similarly, our family of five on a one way ticket to Canada. A container of our household belongings being shipped behind us. Tired after the long flight across the globe to Montreal, the view out the window looked depressing. It was the middle of winter, minus ten degrees with a blanket of dirty grey snow covering the city. We didn't have to say anything. We knew what each other was thinking. "Oh no, what have we done?". But again it turned into another three-year life highlight experience.

And like this new adventure, there would eventually be a turning point to this new challenge. And true to that it soon turned into a fantastic time. My new home for the next few months didn't exactly have the city of Perth outlook. There was no endless view from the balcony or tranquil city lights glistening across the river. Instead, situated right in the heart of this ancient old town, from a typical Spanish style standing room only balcony. Four floors up, the view extended a whole three metres across the narrow street. But what a buzz.

It was a typical night. The clock was just shy of striking twelve as I was making my way home. You could be forgiven for thinking this place doesn't sleep. The streets are abuzz with festivities and there's not even a fiesta on. Tucked in and around the myriad of tiny lanes and streets, people are wining and dining. On this one particular night, the streets, including right below my apartment, are filled with strolling musicians. In traditional Spanish dress, serenading to a cheering and clapping crowd. All this can only explain the culture of the need to take a long siesta for most of the afternoon! But it's clear you do have to get up no later than 8am. That's when the church bells start ringing. Eight long and loud bangs of them.

It's always an exciting challenge arriving in a new city and get your bearings to find your way around. Especially when you're told there's a river, but it's not a river. People would refer to it as the river. I could see the river on the map; it showed a sizable river

CHAPTER 6: Spain. Quality Not Quantity

circumventing half the old city. But no matter where I looked, I could not find the river. I found what possibly could have been a river, but there was no water. It turns out there is no river, but they call it a river. I later learnt, back in the fifties they drained what was the Turia River and turned it into this now continuous stretch of parkland.

I can understand their thinking. It's dense urban living here. Everyone lives in apartments. The kids want to kick a footy around. And if you can't have a backyard for a barbecue... well let's make one, they would have thought. And make it they did. A huge one. It's a fantastic long stretch of continuous recreational parklands. Ten kilometres of uninterrupted cycling path together with throngs of joggers, picnickers, soccer fields, water features and lots of parkland areas.

Singing and dancing in the streets. It's party time in Valencia...again.

What a brilliant idea. Clearly, better usage value for the same space than a few people paddling up and down in little rent-a-paddle boats. But clearly, it's not something we would want to do in Oz. Take the Swan River in Perth city for example. Sure, it has a massive though hugely underutilised area that has nothing more than a ferry going back and forth all day. You could drain it. And yes, it'd be big enough even to run a grand prix on it. But no. I believe we have a touristic obligation to feed the expectations of our international visitors. You see, everyone overseas it seems, is awed by the endless list of things in Oz that can take you out. From sharks, spiders, crocodiles, snakes, you name it, it's there waiting to get you. Yep, we've got the whole package.

So rather than drain the likes of the Swan, instead we need to create a lasting memorable experience. So, fill the river with more sharks. And of course, on the river's edge we'd need to train a few kangaroos to be jumping up and down the mall to meet more foreigner expectations. Add in a few of the other nasties and top it off with a certificate saying, "I survived Down Under".

But back here in Valencia, the experience is certainly a much different one. You could be excused for thinking Valencia is limited to this exciting old town. Not so. The old river has given birth to not only extensive park lands, but at one end, the impressive City of Arts and Sciences. It's an entertainment based cultural and architectural complex. An amazing contrast of very futuristic looking buildings. The river may be void of water, but it's certainly filled with a large abundance of life.

There was a very interesting observation I noted about my experience in Valencia. And it was nothing to do with the place or the people. It was me. I set out on this journey to be unstructured. No routines. Coming to a new place is exciting and stimulating. But what's the first thing you do? Establish routines. This observation first stood out to me when our children were born. I used to think little children would be so flexible. But as soon as they were born, I noted the exact opposite. It's as if we are wired to automatically demand order. We all know what the outcome is when a child's routine is disrupted. Of course, they can adapt far quicker than adults…into another routine.

That's exactly what was happening here. I discussed this observation with a friend, Pablo, who had just moved to Valencia at the same time. What we found ourselves doing was finding the quickest paths to different places such as the supermarket.

CHAPTER 6: Spain. Quality Not Quantity

Identifying our preferred places to drink and eat. We were establishing our daily routines. Our instinctive goal was to turn the unfamiliar into the familiar. The motive of course was to make these daily tasks more efficient, so we didn't have to think about them.

You can see how if you let life take over, what starts out as a simple routine to become more efficient, if you let it, will eventually, decades on, become another rut in life. This phenomenon of our minds was once described to me to be like having a flat plain in our brains. We establish little grooves in this flat plain with each new routine. This helps us to navigate our way through this task without thinking next time. Of course, the more we use this routine, the deeper and deeper the rut. It's obviously an excellent way to become highly skilled in a particular task. But for normal life routines, the longer we leave it, the deeper the rut and the harder it is to get out of it. Hence the need to regularly create new routines. After all, who wants to get stuck in a rut?

At least my visa here wasn't about to let me get stuck in a rut. Plus, there was so much going on in the city. The weekend squares are typically filled with a whole variety of activities. But if you've ever thought someone needed to get a life, spare a thought for this guy. I was peddling the treddly through nearby Plaza de la Virgen. It's a very popular part of town. It's a big open public space. At one end is this statue that looks more like a huge fossilised looking guy taking a bath. He's there day or night I've noticed…whatever floats your bath I guess!

Lined with open air cafes at one end, the plaza is always bustling with people. It also tends to attract the arty types. What caught my eye was this small mound of sand right in the middle of the plaza. So, there's this guy with a teaspoon. He looked a bit arty, so I assume it's in the name of "art". There he is slowly shuffling back and forth shifting the pile of sand from one side to the other, one teaspoon at a time. He's moving at snail pace carrying his tiny spoon as if it had an egg on it. Now I like art, don't get me wrong. But seriously, he would have had to get permission to do that, surely?

I thought about giving him a hand or at least offering him my bike to help get his job done a bit quicker. But he was clearly "in the zone" without the need for my help. I never got back to see if my friend managed to shift his pile of sand. But I could relate to where he was coming from. I've had a bit of closet interest in art too.

I've never really considered myself an artist. But then again, if you ride a bike from A to B, it's quite accepted to be called a cyclist. So, I guess on that basis, if you can hold a paint brush you could be called an artist. Actually, my first foray into the art world was more by necessity. I ordered a dozen prints from China to cover the bare walls of our apartment. Unfortunately, it was not long after we noticed some of the night scenes were starting to turn to day. By three months, all the prints had this rather pasty washed out look. To save face from what was such a fantastic bargain, I decided to give the now completely washed out prints a brand new look. A more arty look. By the time this little exercise was finished, Blue Poles was no match.

But the real pièce de résistance de art was not so much with a paint brush. It was an exhibit at a community fundraising sculptures exhibition. It was at the peak period of climate change hype and when southern Australia was in the grip of a ten year

CHAPTER 6: Spain. Quality Not Quantity

drought. "This is what we can expect from now on", said the climate change experts. So, I created a climate change tank. It was made out of steel mesh, which meant you could stick your fist through it. It wasn't able to hold water. But "amazingly", there it stood all day filling this kettle with water. I was hoping it may have been acknowledged in a science journal. But alas, that was not to be. But it did at least score a decent mention in the World Sculptures News magazine.

My contribution to the world of sculptures art was on a roll. Next year's entry was by far the biggest contribution to circumventing climate change. The Climate Change Fan Farm. The need to cool the planet was reaching hyper stage. Well, you've got me to thank. I dressed up what was a very simple solution, again as "art". But the secret was just a household fan. Not one, but as many as I could find. Perched on pedestals to give it a bit of an arty look, the fans were positioned on the foreshore pointing out to sea. I'm convinced I did as much as anyone to help cool the oceans and therefore abate the onset of doomsday. Some may disagree. But the World Sculptures News magazine that year obviously again saw something in it.

But right now, in Valencia, there was much more happening around the city than trying to solve climate change. On just about every corner was an artist's painting. Buildings and architecture was the common subject. I can see where they're coming from. To me, whenever I have heard a place described as full of architecture, I've always developed this bit of a yawn. Boring. But rather than the academic connotations it's always conjured up in my mind, it's actually the opposite. Living within one of the oldest cities in Europe with all its architecture of a bygone era, creates a fascinating feeling of being taken back into a completely different past world. Add in all these arty characters, whether it's shifting piles of sand with a teaspoon, painting, or filling the different corners of the city with music, brings it all so much to life.

People would often ask me whether I saw this or went there in Spain. I typically answered no. My aim was to experience the local culture and meet interesting local people. If I was achieving that, why go sightseeing for the sake of it? The furthest I ventured away from all that was going on in Valencia, were day hikes. I loved hikes. It was a great way to meet interesting people and discover things about the country side.

It was my third hike in Spain. We could see the distant location of our first trek a few weeks back. No doubt inspired by Hollywood, emblazoned on the side of this distant mountain we had previously climbed, was "Cullera". I was always amazed no one had ever heard of this place when I told them where we went. It's a very popular beach side holiday destination. I Then found it's not that it didn't exist; it's just no one had ever heard of the way I pronounced it! That simple little place name reflects so much of what is "fascinating" about Spanish. Pronounced "Cull-ee-rah"? Wrong. Try "Koo-yeh-daaah" with a soft "d".

Brilliant idea, though. Painting the name on the side of your famous rock. Australia should definitely do the same thing. Not many people you meet overseas know our famous rock is now known by its Aboriginal name, Uluru. I noticed in the local science museum, they still refer to it as Ayers Rock. I have a suggestion. I understand name changes can take a while to get through. So why not do the same as the folk at Cullera did with their rock. On the side of our rock, we paint the words "Uluru". There'd be no question about the name then. Plus, you'd see it for miles.

I did a lot of hikes on this trip. I like walking. But I never realised thirty years ago, just five words could have such a lifelong impact on my family. We used to regularly go on walks. In reflection, maybe my parental judgement skills about our young children's physical ability at the time were questionable. Turns out my encouraging words, "just around the next corner" has left them a lifelong distaste for walking.

Shame really. Because they could possibly miss out some day also meeting the likes of this crazy but fun bunch of Brits and other nationalities, as I did. They call themselves Hash House Harriers. They're all over the world, but here they describe themselves as a drinking club who have a running problem! Most un-Spanish. But then again, going for an eight kilometre run (or walk for those who choose) after a couple of beers is another challenge I never thought of. And not to mention the ritual round of drinks after!

There were no pre-beers on this hike. We were two thirds into our hike. Confronting us was a steep drop-off down the side of a mountain. I was starting to appreciate that perhaps Spain could actually be one of the most mountainous countries in Europe. Some claim it to be the most mountainous after Switzerland. Regardless of which claim is correct, right now we had a choice. We turn back, or we tackle this challenge that lay immediately below us. One slip and we would end up tumbling down the mountain side, bouncing off rocks and bushes as we went. The emerging consensus was to split the group. Those who wanted to risk it and those who chose to take the safe route to go back the same way. I could feel the fear of the consequences building. One slip and all the aspirations of this year long trip would come to a grinding halt.

It was risky. But more often than not, slightly changing tactics provides a simple solution. In the end our hands and rear end got more of a work out, but it couldn't have been a safer descent. No one turned back. Staring down that mountain side, contemplating the options, provided a similarity to many of life's various challenges. Our fears are often greater than the actual challenge.

There is one fear you will be relieved to find you don't have to worry about here. The Mediterranean. A pleasant twenty minute bike ride from the heart of the old city takes you to the enticing beaches on the Mediterranean sea. But it's clearly not a proper sea. There's nothing there to eat you. What an odd experience. Swimming without fear of sharks or even crocs? What is this place? It may lack the white sand of Aussie beaches, but the seemingly endless stretch of beach goes a long way to make up for it.

Home to the 2007 and 2010 Americas Cup, modern hotels contrast against the old heritage looking buildings, typical of an old bygone era port town. It's a delightful stroll and treddly ride along this bustling sea front. Particularly on weekends which bring to life the vibe of this long coastal strip with beach sports, even outdoor tango dancing and all the buzz from the strip of café restaurants.

With an endless choice of bars and cafés, it's clear the Spanish enjoy their wine. It's no surprise; Spain is the most widely planted wine producing nation in the world and the world's third biggest wine producer. No wonder. They've been at it for a few years. Apparently, vineyards dating back two thousand seven hundred years have been unearthed not far from Valencia. Interestingly, Australia only ranks as the fifth wine producer in the world and produces a third of what is produced by Spain. I was born in the

CHAPTER 6: Spain. Quality Not Quantity

Barossa Valley, South Australia, arguably Australia's birthplace of wine. I feel this has given me a strong birthright connection to vino, particularly when served in a glass. As such, an opportunity to experience the Bodegas Mustiguillo winery about an hour's drive away in one of the local wine regions, was a natural given.

Like many of life's true pleasures, there's a certain ritual one has to first go through. The same for a wine tour before one can experience that first aromatic sip. First there's the history. We didn't get to see that ancient old vine, but there was plenty of history to explain about the region's vines. Then there's the vineyard walk. "The smaller the grape the better. It's the skin where all the flavour and characteristics comes from. Not too much water". Make 'em work for the water they need. Mmm, yeah, that's my kind of thinking.

Then the barrels. We're getting closer now. Oooh, yes. We spot the wine tasting room. Not yet though. There's the room full of wine awards to be admired first. A few more barrels. Another room of barrels. This room's a bit cooler. Stops the wine getting too excited. After all wine needs to learn it's a waiting game. And so do we. Like it's not as if you can just squash a bunch of grapes into a bottle and enjoy its exquisite qualities. No. It's all about patience.

Fortunately, our patience was inevitably rewarded. We politely take our positions at the huge tasting table. Not wanting to look like we were making up for our prolonged patience, each sip is appropriately spaced with our newfound qualified judgement of the wine's qualities. Looking into the glass, holding the glass to the light, bit of a tilt here, a tilt there. A roll here, a roll there. "Ah yes. Definitely from that second vine we passed, don't you think?

And I think the aromas I'm picking up would have been from that last oak barrel, you'd have to agree?" Even if you have no idea, it's always fun playing the wine expert game!

From the vibrancy of life in the old city to the nearby mountains, Valencia has it all.

Chapter 7

HEY, LET'S JOIN THE EU

There has been a lot happening on the world stage. What with the likes of the Brits and their friends across the Atlantic wanting to go back to the good old days. Building walls and shutting their doors to the rest of the world.

Shame really. We're going to miss them. So counter trend. The world has become amazingly small. Technology and communications have brought us unbelievably close. Just the ability to video chat across the globe like we're next door, in itself makes the world so much smaller.

But while the rest of them were in the process of getting votes to shut their doors, I said to our Prime Minister, let's join the EU. They've really got a great setup. Each EU nationality can freely move across each country. No visa hassles. Let's face it, we all originate from this lot over here anyway. The Brits (surely they'll change their mind after they realise it was just a bad dream), Irish, Greeks, Italians, Germans, the Poles, etc., etc. When you think about it, Oz is really just a big European outpost. We're already now a part of Eurovision. So why not officially become one big happy family again. We could spend more time with all our long-lost relatives. And the big benefit is you won't have to worry about being thrown out after ninety days.

And you'd be able to enjoy more of these great Spanish fiestas. Like the Mercat Central (Central Market) one hundred year birthday bash. Could you imagine a hundred thousand people jamming the streets to celebrate the birthday of a market? And this would have to be the only place I know where they let off fireworks during the day. Just for the noise. The louder the better. And why not? Life's too short not to miss any opportunity to get together for another party.

People jam the street by the thousands with smoke and explosions to celebrate their Mercat Central 100 year birthday.

And what better way to finish off the Mercat Central birthday celebrations than by attending a Spanish cooking class? To find out how all this wonderful produce comes together to the dinner plate.

I've always had a basic interest in cooking. In my last single life, I kept my recipes in what I called, my "Stir, Stew and Spew" book. It was my survival guide. A collection of basic home cooked recipes. I've always been a bit of a meat and three vegie bloke. However, if it's cooked in a pot and relatively fluid by nature it was what I called slops. If it was served in a more presentable manner, I'd have a go at passing it off as la gourmet la casserole, or whatever name I could dream up. I generally preferred the more simplistic description though.

The need to further develop culinary skills over the last forty years was not required given the high quality cooking skills I was fortunate to marry into. That is, except for the odd relief period.

CHAPTER 7: Hey, Let's Join the EU

My kids still groan at the memories. Particularly my old SS&S book favourite, the Tuna Casserole (Tuna Slops as I of course, called it). I have one basic cooking flaw. I tend be a bit over generous with some ingredients. The kids still complain about the cayenne pepper burns to the back of their throats.

With most of these cooking classes, even for me it's hard to stuff it up. All the ingredients are laid out with closely followed step by step instructions. I did have one concern with this cooking class I was about to attend though. I suspected this class may be a vegetarian only show. I'm a lover of meat. I considered slipping a piece of meat into my pocket, just in case. Surely, quietly blending in my essential additive to the dish couldn't do any harm.

The class was held in the chef's home. The kitchen bench was lined with just about as many ingredients as you'd find in the Mercat Central. This was going to be a treat. It proved a popular class. The place was filled with enthusiastic cooks, note books in hand. I was the only non-Spanish attendee. I have always enjoyed the odd cooking class here and there. If you need to cook to survive, you might as well make it an enjoyable experience. Plus, there is another benefit; it's also another great way to meet people.

I can report the food looked tasty. It smelled just divine. And I found I didn't need to resort to adding my piece of meat. I discovered how delicious a vegetarian meal can taste. It's all in the spices. But while it tasted fantastic, I had no idea what the instructor said. Like, how to actually make it? It was all in Spanish. My note book was the only one whose pages remained blank. No problemo. It's really quite simple. Just a bit of this and a bit of that. Exactly the way Grandma used to cook.

To improve my Spanish cooking skills, it was clear I needed to understand the instructor. I really needed to work on my Spanish. A person I was about to meet, would provide the answer I needed. I had joined another hike. I always found it an interesting experience fronting up to a new group. I'm sure it's a natural trait where we can be very explicit in our private descriptions of people we first encounter. These thoughts can be quite socially inappropriately judgemental. Thank goodness we have filters glued between our thoughts and our mouth…some of course, better than others. More so, how thankful can we be that technology has not yet tapped into our inner most thoughts? Imagine, having no social filters. What if we went up to someone and said, "wow, that's quite a honk you have planted on the front of your face. Air may be free, but that's ridiculous,". Of course, there is a benefit to this raw, unprocessed first level observation. It's a great way to remember people's names. Experts in this field dramatise such first impression images and associate it with their name. An extremely powerful technique that uses our brain's ability to remember extreme images. But please don't tell people how you managed to remember their name.

Of course, it works both ways. I often used to wonder what some of these "young, spring in their step" lot would think as I turned up to join a group hike. "So, this grey haired ol' dude's joining our hike 'ey. Really. Great. I guess we'll be expected to carry him back". Despite what first impressions they may have enjoyed thinking, physically, I was fortunate. It's not age. It mostly comes down to fitness. I felt privileged I could generally keep up with the best of them.

It was a rare hike you could not find someone to have an interesting chat with, often creating ongoing friendship, or if not,

CHAPTER 7: Hey, Let's Join the EU

contact with. This hike was no exception. We were trekking up the mountainside as we chatted. My fellow hiker was a University lecturer. What she told me would explain the dilemma I found myself in this week.

I had been slowly working on increasing my Spanish vocabulary. My attempts reminded me of my grandkids, when they were about two. How excited they felt with each new word they were mastering. Unfortunately, I was nowhere near their advanced levels. But I had been working on it. I finally thought it was time to test my skills. I went downstairs to the local convenience store. It was late at night. I had been rehearsing all day. I fronted up to the counter. I announced my request. That went well. Yes, I could see I was understood. Until what happened next. She asked a question. I urgently needed to provide a response. Now I don't know if you do the same thing, but when I think intensely, I have a tendency to roll my eyes upwards to one side. Maybe it's some primeval instinct as if by looking to the heavens it will give some divine direction. Unfortunately, it must have been out of hours upstairs. Nothing was coming back. Further, when extreme concentration is required, I have another curious habit. My tongue presses hard up against my right cheek, creating a massive boil like protrusion on the side of my face. I've never had this checked out. I didn't think it fair my family should miss out on what to them has remained an amusing syndrome.

So here I am now in this star gazing trance with a huge boil on my face. I could sense the unease of the situation. Worse, I was sure I could actually hear what she was thinking. "If I don't do something about this, by the time this guy comes up with an answer we'd have shut the shop and gone home!" I understood she had no choice. She sympathetically came back with something I could recognise. It wasn't much. But it was enough English to break the deadlock.

My fellow hiking University lecturer went on. She was explaining how she teaches English to all age groups. What was interesting was her observation. She said how there is a distinct drop off in the learning response rate for people at age forty. In many ways it wasn't really news to me. But the advice is clear. If you are nudging close to forty and you want to learn another language, you need to act urgently. Before it's too late. For the rest of us, there is no excuse. It's just going to take a little longer.

But this wasn't the only time this week I found my eyes reaching up for divine direction, my tongue perched in position, searching for answers. Valencia may feel like a very safe place. However, not so for bikes. If they are not bolted down, don't expect to find them when you get back. The inevitable happened. My bike was securely locked to a pole. It was next to a busy shopping area. It was close to 8pm when I made my way back to the bike. But there, right in front of shoppers, was my bike lock being cut in half with a metal hacksaw. In clear view of everyone. It was obvious, time was of the essence. To cut through this lock and make haste before anyone had time to react. Or worse still the police would arrive.

However, this situation was not your normal slash and grab. The difference was, it was me. I was the one holding the hacksaw. Yes, I know what you would have rightly been thinking. He's not even just over forty. He's well and truly over it. He'd forgotten the lock combination. Regardless of any such unfair judgements, I was on a mission to get this job done and get out of there. My

CHAPTER 7: Hey, Let's Join the EU

chances of explaining my way out of this one, were as good as zero.

 Food and more food. It's also worth celebrating. In a big way.

Chapter 8

ARABIAN EXILE EXPERIENCE

You may recall I suggested to our Prime Minister that Oz should join the EU. Just makes too much sense. Most of us lot 'down under' have European family heritage. Why should we be limited to visiting our ancestors for only three months? It's like saying to one of your kids once they leave home they can only stay for three days within any six day period. Mmm, maybe I can see why they imposed a limit on us visiting our European "home".

All this left me in a bit of a dilemma. I hadn't finished my España experience and I would be outstaying my visa. So, I took a quick trip out of the European Schengen zone.

The flight arrived late in the evening. It was like another world. The taxi twisted and turned its way through a never-ending maze of dimly lit narrow streets. The cobble stoned streets were lined with ancient unkept looking mud brick buildings, casting eerie shadows across our path.

I had checked in quite late in the evening. The guest house manager had provided directions where to possibly find something to eat; I had to stoop to get through the black metal door. My biggest concern was finding this door again. It was at the end of a network of dimly lit narrow streets. As I ventured out, I closely studied the markings on each street that led back to that door. It would only take one wrong turn. I noted the overflowing bins, the undernourished cats scavenging what fell to the ground. The odd stranger seemingly lurking in the darkness. I was told however, it was safe.

Welcome to Marrakech, the top of Africa, Morocco. The unique experience of staying right in the heart of the Medina, the old town. Navigating the streets shared with bikes and motorbikes weaving in and out alongside you. Encountering donkeys hauling their carts. Dodging the street beggars. And the never-ending enticements to "come into my shop". An exciting hustle and bustle of ancient city life. With its array of colours of material, clothing, pottery, pots and pans, brass lights, carpets and rugs. The enticing smell of all imaginable spices. Where survival also seems as much to scam the next unsuspecting tourist. "Wrong way. This way". I was aware of this scam.

But I wasn't prepared for this one. I was exploring my way out from the main souk. A local walking in the same direction offers some helpful advice. "Keep to the right" he politely advises as a never-ending stream of motorbikes haphazardly career past. As the conversation grew, he informs about a special tannery market. Just this weekend. He anticipates any concern saying he's not a guide. No cost. After a short while he advises to follow this other man. "He works in tannery". We walk on for twenty minutes.

Scam bells were starting to tingle. I'm now handed off once again. This time to a man waiting at a door. The scam bells are clanging louder. The Tannery tour begins. An expansive outdoor collection of cement baths with camel and sheep skins in various

CHAPTER 8: Arabian Exile Experience

stages of the leather making process. Fortunately, you the reader, can't smell it. It was bloody disgusting!

One bath, as explained, was full of pigeon poop. Now I don't know about your leather bag. But if the leather originated from this part of the world, you can be assured it's been soaked in pigeon shit. The paint stain on your car duco left from bird droppings helps to explain the bleaching power of this natural resource.

An insider's view of the Leather Tannery, complete with Pigeon poop.

Of course, no tour is complete without ending in the showroom. The scam bells were now on high alert. I politely decline the merchant's kind offer to relax on his couch during his product presentation, along with the customary pot of "complimentary" tea. There's no such thing as a free lunch here. Despite the fact I don't think I could ever look at a leather bag the same way again (or at least I'd smell it first), I didn't have any room in my backpack anyway. Meanwhile my friendly guide was waiting outside, ready, as expected, to demand a fee for this tightly networked "free" service.

Unfortunately, my payment, while a fair amount in local currency for the knowledge gained, was way below my now not so friendly guide's extortionist demands. Thankfully, my map was there once again to get me quickly back to more familiar territory. And yes, as confirmed later, this well executed plot also has a name. The Tannery Scam.

As night set in, the chaos of the souks moved to the huge Jemaa el-Fnaa square. A haphazard collection of musicians beating drums and playing stringed instruments, as people fill the square. The excited crowds continue to grow, encircling their rhythmic beat.

Rows of outdoor food markets come to life. Filing past the eateries are the never-ending line of the relentless watch and bead sellers. But now there's an additional member to this endless queue. Children. Quietly anticipating a share of the food from the tables. I notice a young boy has joined the next table. Oblivious to the generosity of his newfound hosts, nor the world around him. He has just one purpose. Staring only at the plate in front of him. He intently feeds himself as quickly as he can consume it. I later glance over. He is gone.

As night deepens, the chaos and vivid colours of the markets quickly disappear. The abundance of merchandise that overflowed into the tiny streets are gone. The lanes have changed to a dull grey of shuttered up stalls. More prominent now are the beggars cocooned in rugs, braving themselves for the cold winter night ahead. Just one bare hand is visible; enough to collect any meagre offerings.

I tap the metal bar off the black door. It finally opens. The warm and friendly riad hotel manager, Aziz welcomes me in with his cheery smile. "Any longer", he jokes "and I would have had to get the police to find you." The door shuts behind us as the passage opens up to an oasis like, tranquil courtyard setting, typical of the riads Morocco is famous for. The rooms, spread over several levels, have no external windows, except to look over the courtyard. Whether for security or privacy, it is certainly one thing; a sanctuary away from the crazy chaos outside. A relaxing place to sit and chat with other guests. And to brace yourself for the next day of life in the Marrakech Medina.

CHAPTER 8: Arabian Exile Experience

An hour's drive away, the serenity of the Atlas Mountains offers a far contrast to the city life below. A three-hour bus trip away is the popular Essaouira, a beach lover's retreat for surfing, kite surfing and swimming. To get around you can choose between a camel along the beach, or a horse and carriage ride through the city. Or maybe if you have luggage, there's always the donkey and cart.

No doubt, the pièce de résistance of this Moroccan experience was a home cooking class, cooking Morocco's famous lamb tagine with lamb, prunes, apricots, almonds and a whole array of spices. It was something to die for!

And to finish off this "visa exile", a six hour bus trip up to Casablanca travelling in modern coach comfort on modern highways. It was the last day of this Morocco visit. And guess what? Another friendly local who came out of nowhere. I politely declined his kind offer to take me to this special market, just on today!

As the wheels touched down on the tarmac, I felt a sense of ease. The city streets that emerged from the subway metro were clean. No garbage to step around. There was a welcoming feeling of familiarity being back in Valencia. It doesn't take long to unpack a backpack. There were people to see. More mountains to explore. A bike ride to the south to explore the Castle of Xàtiva.

As with all of Europe, there's a fascinating history to Spain. From what is now no more than a blip on the history timeline, different invaders have left their influence. From a seafaring mob called the Phoenicians about 900 BC, then several hundred years later the Romans take over. Another hundred years or so, raiders from North Africa decide to have a go. Then amongst all that give or take, a few hundred years or so, there's the Muslim invasion. They at least brought a lot of prosperity. And so it continues. Even as late as 1936 the assassination of political leader Jose Calvo Sotelo resulted in a significant civil war that ended only three years later. Phew. It's good to be here at a time when no one's invading the place.

Meanwhile, by contrast to the turbulence of history, the glow of Christmas lights spread a calming peace throughout the city. Shoppers, as in any other part of the world, filling the late night shops. Traditional dancers and musicians entertain each passer by. The life size nativity scene presents a central feature in the Plaza de la Reina square along with the huge ornamental Christmas tree. And hidden away in a nearby village, a most impressive model of Bethlehem with its animated characters can be found.

Winter is now setting in. But there's no question the chill in the air is replaced by the warmth of the spirit of Christmas. But Christmas in the air means one other thing. It's unfortunately time to say adiós to Spain. And what an experience it's been. Except for one thing. I still can't pronounce that darn street I lived in. Well I can. But it's just that no one's ever heard of it!

I arrived in Valencia not knowing a soul. But by the time I left I had this great little social group. In fact, my social calendar was busier than it had ever been before I left. I have met some wonderful people. Brits, Italians, Canadians, Americans, Irish, Russian, Dutch, French, etc, etc, and of course, many Spanish people. Until next time, "adiós mis amigos en España".

Madrid provided the final stop over before departing Spain. There must have been a hundred thousand people jamming the streets that last night. The pubs and cafes were overflowing, despite it being freezing cold. I asked someone what was on. "Oh, it's Christmas. Happens every year", she said. One thing is clear. The Spanish clearly love celebrating life.

Experience the chaos of life in Morocco.
A final adios to Spain.

Chapter 9

A WINTER WONDERLAND

It was enlightening to be back in unquestionably one of the world's most iconic cities. Featuring in films that have become part of our lives. Inspiring songs that have created defining moments of our time. And as many would claim at this point in history, the world's capital.

It was my first winter experience in the Big Apple. With several degrees below, ice skating was now the main attraction of Central Park. Bryant Park off 5th Avenue glittered in the evening light as ice skaters, surrounded by Christmas stalls, danced to the sounds of carols. As night set in, the Rockefeller centre transformed into a glistening display of festive decorations and lights. Despite the increasing chill, the pulse of the city that doesn't sleep didn't seem to miss a beat.

Broadway and Times Square may be a pulsating vibrant hub of bright lights and action, but beyond that, you feel a marked contrast, especially in some of the surrounding urban areas that feed into it. The aging subway system is no comparison now to the brand new infrastructures appearing in emerging economies. Perhaps it was the grey shadow cast by the chill of a cold winter's night. But curiously, amongst an otherwise dormant grey and almost depressing looking suburban street, the only action in this part of a Brooklyn neighbourhood, is a mega large laundromat crowded with people.

But bright lights and laundromats aside, I was here for another reason. It had been forty seven years since we first met. We were then pimply teenagers. The Rotary International student exchange program had sent a student from a small village in upstate New York to an even smaller dot on the map in South Australia.

How times have changed. As kids we used to watch Dick Tracy on TV. The fantasy of communicating on that infamous watch is now close to a common reality. Our respective grandkids were now experiencing a Christmas from each side of the globe, in real time via a live video call. One enjoying a Christmas in sweltering forty degree plus heat. While here, there is a white Christmas in sub zero temperatures, complete with a snowperson for each of the grandkids back home. While we have whitened ourselves on top, the world has certainly shrunk in those forty seven years. Sharing the magic of a white Christmas live online, with family back home was something we never would have imagined even Dick Tracy doing.

They don't call Oz the lucky country for no reason. Without question, it's obviously the most advanced country in the whole world. I can speak with authority on this. Spend some time this side of the world and it won't take long to realise it. Consider America. Nowhere near a match. In fact it would surprise most people to find it is incredibly far, far behind. Europe is not much better. Even though it's hard for an Aussie to admit it, our "sex pack in the chilly bin, eh bro," Kiwi cousins across the ditch are even more advanced. And I'm not just referring to our national invention, the Hills Hoist

CHAPTER 9: A Winter Wonderland

clothes line. No. I'm talking about our continuous, consistent leading edge position as the world's most advanced nation. One that leaves every other country in our shadow. Always has. Always will. And none so evident as this time of the year.

While Sydney Harbour blazes with spectacular glory as the clock strikes twelve with each new year, you guessed it. The rest of the world is still sleeping. What makes our advancement so obvious on this occasion each year is when your friends from down under message you in New York wishing you a great night. What the? This part of the world, the so-called global leader, is still stuck a day behind. New Year's Eve hasn't even arrived yet. And this happens every day of the year.

But being an advanced country, comes with much responsibility. It's not something that's taken lightly by the good folk down under. By the time America wakes up, our advanced readiness already knows what sort of day it's going to be. Good, bad or otherwise. But they're there for you. They'll let you and the rest of the world know if indeed it's worth getting out of bed for.

Ok, so America is not and never will be as advanced as the land down under. But it does have one other thing. Unquestionably one of the most, if not the most successful and powerful country of our time. It hasn't achieved that without the collective energy and contribution of its people. One of these people, 96 year old Bob Greene, a successful businessperson in his time, we found him still shovelling snow off his driveway. We sat down together for a chat about his life, the challenges, his successes. There was one

Hear what this 96 year old's one piece of inspirational advice is.

particular piece of inspirational advice I took away. He keeps it on his fridge. "Persistence and determination. These are greater than intelligence and education for success".

Five hours further north is Montreal, Canada; our home for three years, twenty five years ago. I'm now returning once more to remember one of the highlights of our family life. Experiencing life in not just a different climate, but a different culture. Where temperatures can plummet into the minus thirties in winter and peak well into the high humid thirties in summer. And when summer does arrive, you make the most of it. You've only got two months.

And it's not just the extremities of the climate experience. It's the culture. The French speaking province of Quebec. Where the language police ensure an appropriate proportion of French language standards such as signage, are maintained. But in reflection, it's a positive move. Go to any major shopping mall in any city of the world, with all their global brands, they all look the same.

But to hear the Quebec cultural experience with every rich word of spoken French, to see the French influenced villages and buildings such as the winter wonderland in Saint-Sauveur, to spend a day skiing down the nearby slopes, experiencing a few days in a snow-covered country cottage cosying up against the warm fireplace, or simply strolling around the quaint Montreal old town (even though it was minus twenty), is indeed a unique experience to be preserved. The bonus is, do all the same in summer and experience a totally different, yet still unique

Producing an Australian Shiraz wine in the middle of a Canadian winter.

CHAPTER 9: A Winter Wonderland

landscape. Then to top that off with the welcoming hospitality of our old Quebecois friends, makes this visit just as much a treasured highlight as it was twenty five years ago.

 Ever dreamed of a white Christmas, glistening white snow sparkling with brightly coloured fairy lights...

Chapter 10

URBAN SWAGGING

To qualify as a gap year, there's a certain minimum requirement to fulfil. By comparison, you can't say you've really experienced the great Aussie outback unless you've slept in a swag. The awe of laying there wondering what strange creatures you may be sharing the darkened night with.

Same with a gap year. You can't say you've done a gap year unless you've done, what I like to refer to as, urban swagging. That is, dormitory sleeping in a backpacker hostel. It's not much different to sleeping in a swag in the outback. You never know what stranger is lurking around you in the night. Could be any creature who nests for the night in anywhere up to the ten or twelve bunk beds in your room. They may look like you. But just like in the wild they typically make strange sounds during the night…and vice versa! As day breaks, they go hunting for food. They may even try to communicate with you. But sometimes you just can't understand them. And they can't understand you.

I urban swagged a few times. And that's the great thing. It's the interesting people you meet. I would have to say, for me it meant facing up to another one of those uncomfortable moments. Walking into a mixed dormitory full of backpackers younger than your own kids. Thinking to yourself. "Mmmm, ok then…". But if it felt uncomfortable, then I felt I needed to do it. Which I did several times. It may have been uncomfortable at the outset but waking up next morning sitting up on the top bunk, thinking "well, this is pretty cool."

Backpacking though, is flexible. You can choose to urban swag as it suits. As one professional female Gen Y solo backpacker explained, you pick what you feel like. If you want to socialise with other travellers, Backpacker hostel. Want more of a local experience? Airbnb. But if you want to splash out and for more privacy, choose a nice hotel. Leonie, a more mature traveller I know, was in her fifties when she backpacked. She had a simple security strategy. She'd always pick the furthest bunk away from the door. And always on the top bunk. That way if some randy young buck came staggering in late at night, odds were there'd be more choices before he made it to the end of the room. Plus, if the buck did make it to the end and up the ladder to the top bunk, he'd probably be disappointed and promptly retreat, she said!

Certainly, the hostel market predominantly caters to the younger traveller. But while a minority, there are a number of us not so twenty somethings. I did note this lady at the more matured end of the age spectrum. You could tell. Compared to all those around her with their fingers dancing and flitting across their gizmo devices, it was her steady yet determined single finger poking action on her not so slim laptop keyboard that definitely gave her era away.

CHAPTER 10: Urban Swagging

The top hostels are like a backpackers equivalent to a resort. They offer a whole range of facilities. From an entertainment theatre, outdoor garden, dining and lounge areas (with of course, numerous smart phone charging stations), full commercial grade self-catering kitchens and private rooms, as well as all the dormitory rooms. Communal dining areas encourage an opportunity for a chat. And that was the reason my preferred choice of accommodation was hostels (though I mainly chose private rooms). Like caravan parks are to caravan travellers, hostels provide an excellent hub for an exchange of travel information and recommendations with other travellers. Like the guy I chatted with over breakfast. Having a transit stopover in New York City, I was about to leave the North American winter behind. The good thing was he bought my now surplus to requirements, as new, thick, winter coat. Saved me having a garage sale at the airport.

Another popular feature of hostels is the access to excellent value tours. Like Jerry's grand walking tour of NY. A retired teacher, he's been doing them for eighteen years. Like a real Aussie Ocker, Jerry's a New Yorker in the truest sense and quite a character. Excellent value too.

Join Jerry's Grand Walking Tour to experience the highlights of New York.

I don't know where else you'd get a ten hour tour for ten dollars! Between the subway and ferry rides, the relaxing pace covering the ten miles (16km) of walking offers a very informative way to experience some of the great New York City highlights.

New York, New York.
The city that doesn't sleep.

Chapter 11

CENTRAL AMERICA. PLAN B

A seemingly endless array of skyscrapers stretching along the city coastline creates an imposing view. An outlook that would rival the best of the world's cities. Connecting the water's edge to these most modern towers of real estate is an inviting, natural, wide open expanse of lawns, gardens, trees, walkways and cycle paths. Almost unnoticeable between these prominent landscape features is a bustling multi lane expressway. This is Panama City. Capital of Panama, Central America. A small nation of just four million people. A country that connects the north with South America.

From outward appearances, it almost seems at odds this city belongs to a country designated as a third world. Curiously, this definition originally came about during the cold war period. Those aligned with the US, first world. Those with the Ruskies, second world. All the rest, third world. By that definition, guess which country you'd never expect to be a third world country? Austria! Yes, God's own garden, Austria. But clearly that definition has now evolved to refer more to developing countries.

I have however, a simpler definition. The degree of ease you can seamlessly walk the city footpaths. How huge the difference in footpath heights are as you cross from street to street. And more defining, the number of mini sinkhole like footpath hazards. Ones that create fear that one step wrong and you'd never be seen again.

So, by this definition, Panama City starts from the coast as a leading first world class city, with the most modern infrastructure. This includes a subway line (with more to come) that far rivals what you find in the likes of New York. However, venture back beyond the skyline of sky-high cost real estate and you'll find yourself rapidly moving through the second world into a third world zone. That is if you make it without falling into a footpath sinkhole. Unfortunately, this reflects a city with one of the highest income disparities.

Canal de Panama. One of the engineering feats of the world.

But it's a city and country on the move, growing as the central finance and transport hub for Central and South America. A country that attracts high numbers of foreign retirees as well as droves of backpackers who come to enjoy the huge natural diversity the country offers. And central to Panamanian's pride in this progressing country, is the Panama Canal. An impressive engineering feat in its own right.

Panama City was going to be my new base. To replicate the experience of Spain. Quality over quantity. This trip was not intended to be a tick off list as to how many countries could be visited. The idea was to experience the fullness of just a few base locations. For three to four months in each continent.

CHAPTER 11: Central America. Plan B

However, that plan went out the window in Panama. Efforts to find a short term rental in Panama were unsuccessful. Wasting further time looking for a place was not an option. Time for Plan B. Not that there actually was a Plan B, but let's call it that. Plus, the idea of just backpacking through each of the many Central American countries had a growing appeal. So, the suitcase was ditched. It was now just a backpack. And I have to say, what a liberating feeling. A backpack no bigger than carry-on luggage size...well ok just a few little kilos over. And that's how I then travelled for the next nine months. All up, 23 countries later, staying in 122 different places of abode. Not quite the original intention.

Staying in anything from guest houses, hostels, dormitories, hotels, bamboo huts, homestays, sleeping on the floor, in a hammock...and a swag. If I didn't like a place I moved on. If I liked it, I stayed. Anywhere from one night to a couple of weeks.

My Central America adventure was now about to take me from Panama City, backpacking through Panama, up through Costa Rica, Nicaragua, Honduras, Guatemala, Belize, Mexico and with the last two weeks of this leg in Cuba.

It had been a full day's travel. We had now left the Panama mountain village of Boquete. The final connecting bus would take five hours to reach the popular Bocas del Toro island on the Caribbean coast. The bus was chocker block full. The roof stacked high with backpacks. The driver either knew every turn through the winding, narrow, mountain jungle road or was on a tight schedule. Either way, as we surged and rolled around each tight bend it was clear he and his accelerator pedal weren't there just to look at each other.

The jungle was by now starting to look the same. As jammed packed as we were in the bus, I found my thoughts being drawn into a moment of sentimental reflection. You know how certain places stick in your mind? This was one of those times. Maybe it was the monotonous drumming noise of the bus against the continuous blur of the jungle flashing past our window. But as I reflected deeper, I found tears welling.

I fixed my view more firmly out towards my window. As if to hide from being noticed by those around, but more to escape deeper into thought. Reflecting on good times past. The times as a family. All the travels we did together. The many laughs, the countless celebrations, the adventures, the fun times we shared. The pride as a father. And as a husband. The times we relished together, just the two of us. The quirky little things we'd say and do. Those things you secretly share just as a couple. Your soulmate.

It was now so different. The way life had suddenly moved on. And in such a different direction. I recalled that deep period of grief, not that long ago. Confronting the personal changes, the roller coaster of emotions. I guess we all deal with loss in different ways. For me, I read as many books on the subject as I could…if there was Grief for Dummies 101, I would have read it. I switched away from the TV news. Too negative. Instead André Rieu's classical music filled every room in the home. I would wonder what the neighbours would be thinking if they could hear this being played day and night. I remembered, how in some curious way, I found it fascinating to observe through this personal experience, how human nature works its way through this period. The emotional journey we are taken on to slowly bring us through such major life changes.

CHAPTER 11: Central America. Plan B

By now the dense foliage of the jungle was finally revealing glimpses of the coast. It was time to return to reality. If moments of reflection serve a purpose, this certainly provided it. An inner glowing warm feeling. But right now, we were getting closer. The next adventure was about to start. Our destination was just below. An island in one of the tropical archipelagos' nine main islands. Connecting the island to the mainland is the final leg of the journey. A slick twenty minute high speed boat ride to our destination.

It was no more than a couple of minutes' walk from the boat landing where I encountered this man, seemingly from out of nowhere. His distinct, weathered features suggested a local inhabitant. In many ways he reflected the rustic, rambling almost shanty character of this tropical island village. "Eh mun, wanna a smoke?" he softly spoke as he quietly walked by me. Maybe I had a weary day's travel look on my face. But what a friendly place and how thoughtful I smirked to myself. I politely declined his kind offer as I continued towards my accommodation.

The town was about to be home for the next week. Definitely not the sort of place you'd expect to find a five star hotel. But look beyond the unkept, almost ramshackle like appearance and an inviting tropical lifestyle awaits. The main street is home to an endless choice of rustic, no airs and graces, waterfront restaurants. Enjoying a cold beer and meal on a warm balmy night with the twinkle of lights across the harbour dotted with crisscrossing boats, becomes the norm.

And go beyond the slow paced chaos of Bocas Town, hidden nearby on the island or just a short water taxi ride away to the other nearby islands and emerges another tropical life. Along the stretches of white beach sand, nestled amongst jungle greenery, are the sparsely dotted, sea view grabbing homely looking resorts. Or private homes for those choosing a lifestyle away from a normal western life. And extend beyond the coast into the cooler higher regions, you discover a similar range of nationalities living out dreams of a more sustainable life. Or just a great place to live. On the more eco end of the alternative scale, a short bike ride into the island reveals a house being constructed from thousands of plastic drink bottles.

It's now mid Saturday morning as the town starts to come to life. A surf board strapped over the shoulder, the young surfie revs off on his scooter in search of the alluring waves. Another surfie with long board under arm, skates his way down the main street. A couple of old guys zip around the corner on quad bikes. "Walking is for the young" according to another two senior couples casually driving down the main street on another quad bike. Two on the front. Two perched on the back. For us it's five minutes 'island time' before our bus is due to leave for beach Playa de Estrella at the other end of the island. Twenty minutes later we're finally off. But the delay is worth it. Dining on local grilled fish while enjoying a cold Panama beer next to the tropical water on the white sand beach. The background lined with gently swaying palm trees. A delightful tropical treat.

Night fall, another tropical surprise awaits. Night swimming in the Caribbean Sea with fluorescent glowing bio-luminescent plankton. It's a spectacular experience, floating in the middle of the ocean. Look upwards to the galaxy of stars. Look downwards while you move through the water and experience a starry like sky in the dark water from all the tiny glowing specks of plankton.

CHAPTER 11: Central America. Plan B

Of course, there is just one problem. Getting to sleep at night. Swallow too much of that plankton water and every time you roll over you think the lights come on!

Skyscrapers that dominate the skyline. From the city to the mountains. Along the Panama Canal to the idyllic villages on the Caribbean. There's a lot to see in Panama.

Chapter 12

LET'S LEARN SPANISH

I'm convinced you can travel anywhere in the world with not much more than a very limited vocabulary. When it comes to food, a chook is a chook (chicken for those not from down under) and a pig is a pig. Whether it's in the middle of China or the Middle East. If you're stuck what to order for a meal, it's amazing how a few animated animal gestures help communicate.

Fortunately, technology has just about surpassed the need to flap your arms like a chicken or grunt and snort like a pig to order a meal. Mobile apps like Google translator are amazing. For example, posting a letter at the Oficina de Correos (post office). Not knowing what counter to go to, pointing the phone's camera at the sign translates the directions into English on the app's screen. Great in supermarkets as well. It's comforting to know my carton of leche is actually milk.

But of course, to really appreciate the richness of the cultural experience, some understanding of the local language to communicate becomes essential. I did attempt to learn German once. I was a teenager at the time. I must have lost the book soon after I started. Because all I remember to this day is "Ich liebe dich". I think that's why my family were concerned as I was departing on this trip. I had this brightly coloured strap secured around my luggage case. Easy to identify on the carousel, I thought. But as they explained, running around Germany saying, "I love you" with a symbolic striped rainbow coloured strap in tow, could attract more than what I had bargained for! I changed the strap.

Language learning is a thriving business. Spanish is the fourth most spoken language in the world, spoken in forty-four countries (including the US which is the second largest Spanish speaking country). There are an endless number of English and Spanish schools throughout Latin America. There are people who have sold up everything and secured, for example in Spain, a twelve month visa to attend a Spanish language school. More than that of course, is the excitement of a new adventure and cultural experience.

As big, is an extraordinary movement that's called language exchange meet-ups, noticeably in Spain. Every day and particularly at night in bars, somewhere around the city there is an enthusiastic group meeting to improve their language skills. In casual settings of a few people per table, Spanish and foreign expatriates exchange conversation to improve their respective language skills, as well as to meet new friends. It's a very active social movement. Then there are others such as a Brit who went to Spain with the sole intention to learn Spanish. Living only in a Spanish speaking environment, he explained how the completely isolated feeling slowly turned to occasional "ah ha" moments and to gradually picking up the language. Observing him twelve months on with fluent conversations in Spanish was very inspiring.

CHAPTER 12: Let's Learn Spanish

Learning Spanish was never my intent. But I thought I'd give it a go. The first week did not start off well. It was all in Spanish. I couldn't even understand the questions. I'd always been at least in the upper average of any schooling I'd done. Within ten minutes I realised I was unquestionably the dunce of the class. I felt embarrassed. Quietly slipping out the window in the back of the class room seemed like a more attractive option. However, I was assured if I stuck it out it would get better. End of the week, they graciously gave me a refund. I changed schools. I enrolled at an equivalent to a kindergarten for adult Spanish. I started again. All up I did about eight weeks in over 5 countries. I really enjoyed learning it.

One thing people will tell you is a Homestay with a Spanish family is a great way to improve your language. I thought, that sounds like just what I need. Sort of a fast track to a Spanish speaking expert, I figured.

My first experience was in Costa Rica. Costa Rica is described as the Switzerland of Central America. I'm not sure if it's the higher cost, the mountains or the beauty. But it is certainly that, a country renowned for its beautiful natural features. And the friendliness of the Costa Rican people is evident as soon as you cross the border. My quest to add a few more words to my Spanish vocabulary took me to Turrialba, a mountain village in the middle of the country. The homestay is organised by the Spanish school. This was a school with a difference. Each week is a different school location in both Panama and Costa Rica. When I joined the school, they were two weeks into their four week travelling program. It certainly was a lot of fun. Spanish classes by day. Homestay by night.

My homestay home was a typical average house on the outskirts of the town. Houses throughout Central America are pretty well fortresses featuring tall, iron barred fences with well secured gates. It's much the same throughout all Latin America and Spain. I never understood why the need for such a high level of security. The best explanation I got was it's not so much the locals, but the itinerants from across the border. It's the same in the Middle East. Basically, it seems no one trusts anyone else. Or is it because all these countries have evolved from a history of constant invasions over the centuries?

Whatever the reason, it's quite a foreign concept to what we generally experience in the west. Or certainly down under. In particular what stands out are the shops. By day the streets are vibrant and alive, full of people, overflowing with colourful produce and merchandise. Yet by night, the people are gone, the goods stored and shutters securely down. Not a sign of a shop is evident as the market streets transform into almost dark, depressing, deserted laneways. So if we ever complain about our outdoor shopping malls lacking activity at night, at least we have not got to the stage where we need to board our stores up.

This was my first homestay experience. I was driven to what would be my home for the next week. I was about to spend a week in a completely foreign environment. No English. Only Spanish. The gate was now firmly locked behind me. I peered through the solid iron bars of the fence, looking back at the familiar, friendly faces in the car as it was about to drive off. I smirked to myself as it set a scene in my mind as feeling like I was suddenly locked behind bars of some foreign detention centre. But any sinking

CHAPTER 12: Let's Learn Spanish

feeling I started to feel was quickly dispelled by my welcoming hosts.

They were very nice people. The house had all the usual comforts one would expect. A private room with desk. Shared bathroom. There was a downside though. Meals. I normally don't eat a full breakfast every day. I enjoyed a hearty breakfast on day one. For the second day I managed to communicate, just toast would be fine. Problem was every day after that, there on my breakfast plate were just two pieces of toast. Meanwhile they feasted on delicious servings of fruits, cereals, omelettes. I couldn't quite work out how to tell them without offending. So, toast it was every day. Two pieces.

These people were very, very patient. A conversation which would normally take anyone else five minutes, took me at least three hours. But I was starting to feel pretty proud of my Spanish ability. From one conversation I had understood her sister, who lived next door, was unfortunately deaf and mute. I was feeling pretty chuffed I worked that out. As I turned in for the night, I thought, this homestay really works.

Until the next morning. I'm sitting there, with my two pieces of toast. Next, I observe the sister next door chatting away. What the? I couldn't believe my ears. I've just witnessed an amazing overnight miracle I thought. But more likely I sadly contemplated, I had no idea after all what I thought I understood the night before. But there was good news and bad news. The bad news was sister didn't have a miracle healing. The good news was I did understand correctly. Two sisters live there. One has normal hearing ability. The other is deaf and mute.

Learning Spanish can be fun. There's so much to explore at the same time.

Chapter 13

IT'S ALL ABOUT THE JOURNEY

I was developing a love affair. I certainly had never in my wildest dreams anticipated this. It was the last relationship I ever thought I would get close to. But as each week went by, we were spending more time together. We'd been to all sorts of places. We had an adventure across Morocco together. We both travelled between New York and Canada. Now in Central America we've been up mountains, through jungles and down to the coast in Panama, then in Costa Rica. Part of the adventure is the journey. That's why I've now come to love buses.

We were on another outing. Two buses and several hours later we had now travelled from the central mountains of Costa Rica back to near the Panama border on the Caribbean coast. Puerto Viejo, Costa Rica. It's a kind of a surfie dude sort of seaside village.

It's the casual laid back feel that gives this popular seaside place an enticing feel. The palm tree lined beach front sets the scene for enjoying a beer on the balmy warm evenings. A place as if there are no rules. Just a loose understanding of the way things work. Like the main street that weaves its way along the beach front from one end of town to the other. Where the vehicles respectfully navigate around the locals, surfies and tourists casually flip flopping their way around town. With the occasional cyclist dawdling along on their rusty old treddly. Some with surfboards strapped to the side, others just doing their daily thing.

One of the features that seems to define Puerto Viejo are the many bars, cafes and restaurants. They each have their own unique character. Typically, that beachy, rustic feel. But there was one standout to me. Perhaps it was the quirky character of the place that appealed to me. It looked like the joint had been put together over several decades from left-overs of numerous garage sales, then one day randomly doused in different colours of paint. The sort of place you'd expect to be run by some long grey hair in a ponytail hippy type character who's been planted there since the seventies. But despite appearances, an ex international journalist and his wife were running quite a smart business. It's only after I noticed the name, which gave the clue away; Outback Jack. A touch of the Aussie outback in the middle of Costa Rica run by Outback Jack and his wife Penny.

A touch of an Aussie outback in Costa Rica. But it's what Outback Jack had to say I found interesting.

But there's one other thing I will remember Puerto Viejo for. My son had been trying to get me to do this with him for years. But now I felt the stars were finally aligned… no sharks, warm water. Like hey dude, I had my first go at surfing. Spent more

CHAPTER 13: It's All About the Journey

time in the water than on the board. But, hey dude, I did catch a wave for a few special moments. Better still, it was captured on video….as proof.

You can only surf for so long though. It was time to continue the adventure. What I liked about my new love affair with buses, was the adventure. You never quite know where you're going to end up or what to expect.

From my surfing debut village of Puerto Viejo to the capital San Jose, is about a four to five hour bus trip. It wasn't looking good, though. This was not going to be a comfortable trip. I later learnt what the significance of the letters "EN PIE" that were stamped on the ticket was; "Standing Only". I'm not sure who missed out, but I figured if I kept my head down and avoided eye contact with the driver, I would go unnoticed having a seat for the whole trip. It worked.

San Jose is one of those two day tick off places. Despite what the tour guide suggested that people need to stay longer. A pleasant enough stopover, but there was more to see. Next stop, another four hour bus ride to Monteverde. This is a small mountain village in the north central region of Costa Rica. It's renowned for its famous Cloud Forest. Walking trails lead you through the jungle and of course in the clouds. Plus, heaps of wildlife species. So they say. Must have been their day off as I didn't see any. The jungle walk was great. But back in the village it was blowing a gale. I don't like wind. I was happy to move on after just one night.

The next destination was the Pacific coast in the next country up in Nicaragua. And that's where this bus journey brought home the efficiency of this otherwise outwardly appearing chaotic system. And the adventure.

From the best available information, the first requirement was to take the 6am bus from the mountain village down to the coast. But don't go all the way. When the bus crosses the main trans-American highway, get off. It's about a ninety minute ride on an unsealed bumpy road down the mountain. So along with other like-minded travellers, that's what you do. When the bus stops, you get off. You then find yourself on the side of the main highway in the middle of nowhere, thinking, now what?

The next stage however is to look for a bus that's heading your direction, north or south. Amazingly, twenty minutes later a large Nica bus pulls up. This bus now provides near plush comfort as it heads north. Several hours later, we are at the border. Waiting around at the border, the locals offer further clues how to get to our beachside destination. A half hour further north, now in Nicaragua, the bus pulls over. Once again, we're on the side of the road thinking, now what. As the bus takes off, it reveals on the other side of the road, a Chook Bus.

A chook bus is actually known in Latin America as a Chicken Bus (chook is the Aussie translation for chicken). A chook bus refers to the fact these buses are often crammed with passengers not unlike a truck load of chooks. And that I can vouch for. As the bus fills, it's game on. The aim of the game is then to see how many human chooks can be crammed in through the back door of the bus.

A chook bus is typically an old retired yellow school bus from North America. You get a sense there's a lot of pride operating these classic machines. That is if the number of times the driver blasts the air horn at every slight opportunity is any indication. Back in Panama City, running a chook bus is taken to a new level.

CHAPTER 13: It's All About the Journey

It's there where you find these old relics looking more like a well decorated graffiti machine on wheels, kitted out with a mandatory set of massive dual chromie exhaust stacks jutting up the back.

A chook bus generally works with a team of at least two people. Firstly, there's the driver. You can see his passion for the job by his personalised cabin space. Complete with tassels, little decorations and personal pictures mounted around the dash panel. More noticeable is the glow of pride on the driver's face that reflects a certain status of him and his chook bus. Then there's the side kick guy. He's clearly subordinate to the driver. He glances at the driver with a look of awe and respect. The side kick guy controls the door. He will jump out the door, even before the bus comes to a halt, yelling out to announce their destination. This is not done with the almost near death like slow movement you find in your typical bus employee back home. No. This is more like the hyperactive passion of someone on speed. Someone who unquestionably loves their job.

So back on the highway. There we were stranded on the side of the highway for the second time. With the coach just back on the highway, our sinking feeling of now what, is suddenly interrupted. But this is where the magic happens.

There's loud yelling from the old yellow chook bus across the road. We realise they are yelling at us. And gesturing at us to get on board. What the? "How do they know where we want to go?" I ask my final leg fellow travellers.

I can confirm the reason for the name, chook bus. The bus was chocker block full. Not just seats but every available standing room space. But a chook bus driver and his sidekick clearly like a challenge. As if each journey is a Guinness book of record attempt as to how many people they can cram into a vehicle. I was convinced we were about to enter one of these records. The bus obviously had a time schedule to meet. Our backpacks were literally thrown onto the roof. There were already bodies crammed up against the back door. But this was obviously going to be a new world record as it was clear there were still remaining air pockets to be used.

It's all about the journey. Before we knew it, with bums and armpits and all in faces, we were at this delightful seaside village of San Juan del Sur.

From the Caribbean coast to high in the mountains. Getting there is half the fun.

Chapter 14

TRAVEL – IT'S ALL ABOUT THE PEOPLE

I had only intended to stay a couple of days. That's the great benefit of having no set itinerary. If you like it, you stay. If you don't, you move on. Travellers will say how you get a certain feel for a place. If you connect with it or not. San Juan del Sur was one of these places. There was a certain social vibe about the place. It's a popular destination for North American expatriates. They live here either permanently, or for a few months as part of an annual migration pattern. It's also a popular destination for the young backpacker. Which implies a good party scene. That includes the nearby surf beaches being an additional draw card.

Two days turned into two weeks. It all started with a Rotary Club International sign outside one of the restaurants on the main street. I made myself known when I turned up for their next meeting. I had only been in Rotary for five years. That's quite a newbie compared to many members who count their membership in decades. The San Juan del Sur club was a relatively new club. It seemed to have escaped the usual rigid meeting protocol that decades old clubs appear to enjoy clinging onto. These members were a mix of predominantly North American expats and Nicaraguans, which certainly made the meeting interesting. Every part of the discussion was translated. When a Spanish speaker had something to say, it was translated to English. And vice versa. Your typical Rotary meeting usually goes for an hour. It seemed logical to me this meeting should be allowing at least two hours!

But there was a standout quality about this new club. It's the impact, the difference they were making to this local community that caught my attention. It may be a fledgling club. But you'd never know. This small club is a powerhouse of activity serving their local community. In a big way. For one, it's a central coordination hub for volunteering groups of senior high school kids from the USA.

Each group takes on a school. It's like a version of the property makeover TV shows. They'll paint all the classrooms inside and out, erect water tank stands, install plumbing. Then a week later leave not only a pristine looking school, but grateful pupils and their teachers. But more so, there's a bus load of young people heading home, their lives so much more positively changed from the experience.

Similar programs operate in Oz. For example, one is organised by the Mill Point Rotary Club in Perth. Instead of the annual Schoolies end of year drink to get drunk fest, a group of school leavers go to Laos to work on similar projects. Nothing wrong with a few drinks and a great party, but I wonder who comes home richer for the experience?

CHAPTER 14: Travel – It's All About the People

While local schools were getting a makeover, another exciting project was happening. One that has far reaching implications to the local community. I spoke to one of the local people. Silvana was talking about her family. She sketched on a piece of paper the relationships of each sibling and their children. I asked her why her brother's name was missing above his list of children. "Diving accident" she went on to explain.

It is reported there are up to ten to twenty diving fatalities each year in Nicaragua. Using only a car air compressor on a boat feeding unclean air to a diver below using not much more than a garden hose is not a good start. These divers are then going down to hazardous depths, without training on the dangers and precautions. Deaths are attributed to the deadly "decompression syndrome". The root cause is desperation. The need for fishermen to make a living, to feed their families.

It's a worldwide plight. As fish stocks are depleted, fishermen need to go further out. Without enforced fish management controls, the cycle continues with ever shrinking numbers of available fish. And that's exactly what's happening in this small fishing community. Divers are forced to go further out into deeper water to fish for the high value lobster. And it is increasingly coming at a high cost of life.

But one man has a mission to change this cycle. A Belgian plumber. I met him at the Rotary International Club.

The Belgian plumber, Christian Poseidon, is one of the main coordinators of these activities. But his real passion, along with his enthusiastic fellow team members, is making a difference by what happens under water. Creating artificial reefs. The team is aiming to encourage marine life closer back to shore. Including lobsters.

While the outcome of this project is still at a developmental stage, it is attracting significant support from global funding sources to expand his work.

The team is also collaborating with research centres around the world. Through a personal contact in this industry in Australia, I was pleased to have the opportunity to introduce one such resource through the University of Tasmania. As well, there is growing interest in this project from other communities to replicate the benefits of not only generating increased fish stocks, but also providing diving tourism benefits at these new reef sites.

Belgians it seems, must have a passion for preserving marine life if the work of two Belgians in San Juan del Sur is an example. Another inspiring Belgian was a person I had the opportunity to spend a day with. But it is what she discovered that day that got her really excited. I had joined one of their dolphin and whale surveys in San Juan del Sur. The program is an initiative of a young Belgian marine biologist, Joelle De Weerdt. It's run purely by volunteers.

Dolphins are truly amazing creatures. Witnessing these majestic marine creatures playfully speeding alongside you is a special experience. In front of the boat, darting underneath, across and around. It's hard to tell who's enjoying it more.

Then to experience all those other majestic creatures of the deep. The whales, pounding up and down in and out of the ocean. There must have been at least fifty of them. That was until Joelle politely pointed out it was the same pod of four whales. It's just that they reappeared at different locations. It's an acquired skill to identify individual whales I soon learnt.

CHAPTER 14: Travel – It's All About the People

But the real excitement on this survey mission was when Joelle and her crew discovered something very special. Whale poo. To you and I, it would just look like a bit of murky water. But to Joelle and her team, they couldn't get it into their test tubes quick enough.

San Juan del Sur was going to be a just a few days stay. Discovering so much going on there and meeting interesting and inspiring people led to a longer stay. Plus, it's a fun sort of town…

There is much more to Central America than just lobsters, water, whales and dolphins. Central America is hot. I'm not just talking about the air temperature. But what's just below the surface. There are 109 volcanoes in the region and 16 just in Nicaragua. That number does seem to vary widely depending on who you talk to. Regardless, there's enough of them there you'd have to wonder if the place could one day go off big time.

We miss out on volcanoes down under. So I thought, no better opportunity to check one out. I joined a trekking tour on the island of Ometepe. It boasts two volcanoes on the one small island. You can drive around the island in a few hours. Though not recommended on the scooter I had. Poor thing must have wondered what hit it with some of the off the main road tracks I took it on.

I chose the biggest active volcano to tackle. 1600 metres up. Slight misunderstanding though. I thought it was a five hour return trip. Wrong. Five hours up and five hours down. With steep climbs through tropical growth tracks to slippery volcanic stones near the top. It proved quite a gruelling day out. Leg muscles days after were still complaining. Near the top, tiny droplets of water that clung to every hair follicle, reminded us we were in the clouds. But unfortunately, that also meant all our efforts to see inside the volcano would not be rewarded. Visibility was just several metres. It's all about the journey anyway, not just the destination. Right? But there was no question it was active. You could smell the sulphur. And in places near the top, a number of rocks were too hot to touch.

After that demanding experience, I thought that's it for volcanoes. Tick that one off. Until I arrived in Granada. Volcan Masaya, I was told has real lava, and get this, you can drive right up to the top. So that's what I did. It's a popular attraction, which means the queue at the base of the volcano can take an hour or two. The gates open near nightfall to make the view into the volcano spectacular. You're not disappointed. Real, hot red lava. And I only had to walk twenty metres from the car to the rim of the volcano.

One of the fascinating things about travel is the people you meet. But on this occasion, there was a special surprise waiting for me. Someone I wasn't expecting to see. I met this lovely Canadian couple in Nicaragua. We became good friends. We met on a boat tour of the Isletas de Granada in Granada. Before we even knew each other, she said to me later, "you were not alone". Unbeknown to me, there was someone sitting next to me on the boat tour, she explained. That's interesting, I thought. There were only the three of us on this small tour that I could see.

It was my wife, I was told. The ability to connect to past lives is a fascinating area. That wasn't the first time meeting someone with this psychic gift. To me, you can't prove it and you can't disprove it. So, since there's a choice, I choose to believe it. Why? Because it provides a positive good, comforting feeling.

CHAPTER 14: Travel – It's All About the People

Now I don't suggest I was always one hundred percent the most attentive husband. So, to you my wife, if I didn't notice you sitting next to me, I'm sorry. But it was very nice of you to come along. You certainly picked a lovely part of the trip to join me. It certainly was a lovely tour with our boat taking us around all those dozens of small lush green islands. I know you would have loved, as I did, being surrounded by all those tranquil sheltered water ways. Wasn't it interesting how some islands are only big enough to accommodate just one house? There may be many quite basic homes, but did you see all the other islands big enough for multiple homes? Then all the very palatial homes. It was a lovely day out with the new friends you introduced me to. Thank you. I'm sure you would agree it's a must do tour if anyone is visiting Granada. But I guess you can't expect there will always be a spare seat!

Oh, and one other thing. I am so sorry. Had I known you were next to me, I would have wished you happy birthday. Of course, it was actually your birthday, Australian time, when you joined me on the boat. That made it even more special. Happy Birthday! There's no denying it's comforting to know someone from your past life has dropped by to join part of your journey. Especially on their birthday! But for the here and now, having the ability to connect with so many people along the way is very special. To share the journey with, even if briefly.

There are a number of options. The day tours being one, as with this experience. Language classes have proved a great opportunity to meet people and make friends. Typically, people in the same situation. Then there's a range of mobile apps. Before arriving in a new city, several apps are a great source of finding potential functions to meet people. For example, an international event in Peru, coincidentally turned out to be a good birthday party. The majority of the hikes, a great way to meet people, can be sourced through online social groups.

That little handheld device is not just useful for checking your Facebook updates. It's like mission control for travelling. Online maps to find your way, apps to manage your ATM travel card, booking apps to find a bed, social calendar apps to connect with other people, travel guides for research, etc. It's hard to imagine what travelling was like without it.

There's so much going on in Nicaragua. These photos help to tell the story.

Chapter 15

IT'S DANGEROUS. BUT I WENT ANYWAY

I have lost count of the number of times people have said, "Central America. Isn't it dangerous"? Even in Panama, I was advised not to venture further north than Nicaragua. "It's too dangerous", I was told. Noticing people were going into Honduras, the next country up, and making it back, I figured it can't be too bad, so I went anyway.

Had I not, I would have missed out on this island paradise with its tropical waters and beautiful beaches shaded with palms against a background of mountains. As one Texan explained, it's North America's Bali equivalent to Australia. Roatan island is a small island off the coast of Honduras on the Caribbean.

What's different about Roatan is it offers a range of resort type quality accommodation, particularly in the popular West Bay area. Not the high rise over-commercialised type, but typically set back, hidden amongst beach front palms. Choose between a range of bars and restaurants along the beach strip. Or be enticed by the aroma of barbequing chicken on a street stall and find yourself being ushered to dine at a makeshift table setting on the beach under the palms. Further along the island is the main town of Coxen Hole. Not that it's a hole of a place as the name may suggest. Rather it offers more of the original, authentic character of the island with the traditional street market stalls and cafes.

No chook buses here though. Getting around the main part of the island is simple and cheap…once you work it out. Otherwise you're sitting game for taxis that will have you paying anywhere up to quadruple the local rate. My favourites are the eighteen seater vans that transverse the main part of the island every ten minutes or so. I don't think these vans were ever designed for public use. Particularly the side sliding door. The door seals are well and truly a thing of the past, having endured an unrelenting number of times being slammed open and shut, each time screaming a dull, painful raw metal to metal sound. While its glory days of a normal door are long gone, it does however at least provide a barrier to stop people falling out. It does the job, adds to the character of island life and all for less than a buck.

While the West End offers more upmarket standards of accommodation, I chose the more down to earth appeal of a backpacker hostel. A good hostel offers a great social community. The first night on the island was a bonfire and dinner on the nearby beach. It's also a great way to connect with others. To share information on where and how to get to places. Or like a randomly organised mini United Nations visit to the east end of the island. There was a Brit, Yank, Canadian, El Salvadorian and me, the Aussie. If you don't want to rent a car from the majors, do what Dan the Brit did. Meet a guy in the street. Pay him fifty bucks, no paperwork and drive off for the day in his as new Toyota. What the…?

One of the popular attractions on Roatan Island, and perhaps more so, neighbouring Utila Island, is diving. Many people come

CHAPTER 15: It's Dangerous. But I Went Anyway

here to advance their diving qualifications. Qualifying as a Dive Master is one of the popular ways young people use to see the world and get paid for it. For the rest of us, like me, diving is a pleasant occasional recreational activity.

There is certainly something unique about floating effortlessly metres underwater, being at one with hundreds of fish swimming around you. I first learnt to dive in the Cook Islands. That was the start of a string of, well let's just say interesting, dive experiences. It was my first dive. And it's where I found myself abandoned by the dive instructor. Unbeknown to me, he discovered his boat's anchor had broken loose. His boat drifting out to sea clearly had higher priority, while I was left to find my own way back to the surface…and the drifting boat.

A more memorable dive experience was in northern Queensland with my son-in-law. In fact, he wasn't even a son-in-law at the time. And that was the problem. He had taken myself and mate Tony to one of the local, popular dive spots. We went down while he stayed in the boat, or so we thought. Visibility proved to be extremely low and before we knew it, we were being swept out to sea. Next stop China. Thankfully, by chance one of his mates was passing by and rescued us. Where's Pete we wondered? This is where it gets interesting. We find Pete back on shore schmoozing, not the daughter, but daughter's mother. Smart guy really. Work on the mother first, then the daughter. For us, I guess it was a small price to pay for getting a top son-in-law!

The biggest problem with diving can be the "occasional" bit. Such was a dive a couple of years back. It was in Bali. I hadn't dived for seven years prior. I'm always a bit apprehensive before a dive anyway. Being amongst a group of other divers, it's easy to first assume they are all experts. So, of course one tries to look cool, aiming to project an air of competency. Then also trying to do a quick mental revision of what hose goes where, can all mount to added anxiety.

However, looking cool doesn't always equate to knowing what you are doing. Thankfully, son-in-law was extremely polite as he discreetly pointed out I had the wetsuit inside out. It was very nice of him. But unfortunately, my oversight for detail didn't stop there. In front of everyone, about to put my gear on, he had to point out, again with much discretion, that this time I had the zip at the front instead of the back.

Of course, any subsequent dives I find myself being highly attuned to my diving wardrobe. As was the case now in the Roatan Island Dive centre. Once again trying to look competently cool. And what do they do? They totally confuse me. They hand me a wetsuit with the zip on the front.

After enjoying the diving and several days of island life, there was more of Honduras to explore. An hour and a half ferry ride on a modern as any ferry you'd find, brings you to La Ceiba on the mainland. After an overnight stay and a 4am rise, it's back on the bus. Nine hours later in the comfort of a, well excuse me... "Executive Plus" seating section of a trans-national bus, to Copan Ruins near the Guatemala border.

The ruins go back to the Mayan era. Not wanting to bore you fellow non-archaeological folk, but suffice to say this Mayan mob had a pretty good setup. They lasted for about sixteen Kings and a population of about twenty five thousand people. Mind you, that was well before our time of course. Like back about two and half thousand years. Then it was all over for them. Ran out of

CHAPTER 15: It's Dangerous. But I Went Anyway

food apparently. By contrast the Spanish only turned up about a thousand years later. But they mainly just wanted to pillage all the gold on the continent and get everyone to talk Spanish. Maybe I'm not a good judge of character, but when I was in Spain they seemed like really nice people? Just doesn't make sense. Anyway, wasn't any gold in Copan, so they went straight past. So poor ol' Copan lay forgotten up until just a couple hundred years ago. The Spanish sure missed out. Because if they had known, they could have enjoyed the likes of a weekend we enjoyed with a music band and a parade in the town square.

Now admittedly Honduras doesn't have a reputation as the safest place, but pick your spots and there's a lot to experience and enjoy. Moving further north through Central America, is Guatemala. If you are looking at picking up some Spanish, their schools are probably the best value in Latin America and Spain. It's here where you can experience some of the best of Central America.

It's the start of another day in Panajachel, Guatemala. The streets are already bustling with activity. The woman cooking tortillas gestures a cordial "Hola, Buenos Dias". The local market, just a few minutes' walk down the rough cobble stoned road brings the assortment of traffic from pedestrians, trucks, vans, tuk tuks, bicycles, motor bikes and cars, to an almost halt. The pickup trucks stop to unload their produce, their tyres bulging from the overload of fruit and vegetables or baskets of chickens. There's crisscrossing of people in all directions. Women with babies strapped to their back as they carry their goods perched effortlessly on their heads. Men carting produce into the market with wheelbarrows you'd expect to only see in an antique shop.

Hunched over backs laden with heavy sacks of vegetables, baskets of live chickens or anything that needs moving.

Just beyond the market, the Catholic Church provides a major landmark and focal point as it does in all the surrounding villages. The bustling flow of traffic quickly takes you further along the road as it narrows into a colourful, lively street. Lined with stalls selling anything from the abundance of locally produced hand woven brightly coloured fabrics, bags, clothes, to bars, restaurants and coffee shops. People casually meandering along. Tuk tuks as if playfully bobbing up and down along the street. Its little wheels bouncing between each cobblestone as it revs and shuffles past.

Drawing you further through the street, the water's edge of the lake provides an almost tranquil contrast. The misty clouds around the far perimeter of the lake, as if intentionally, lightly veil the hidden, powerful majesty of the surrounds. Reaching up through the clouds reveals three massive volcanoes towering over the lake's edge. You can't help but feel a surreal sense of fragility. That nature, as much as it can provide, can just as quickly take away. For where you are now standing was once also an active volcano. This vast tranquil lake now gives life to the several quaint villages dotted around the inside rim of the old volcano walls. With each village offering its own unique character. From spiritual lifestyle themes offering yoga and healing, to a huge array of arts and crafts. Another catering to the backpacker adventure seekers. Life inside this volcano is truly one of nature's gifts.

The form of transport in these countries is interesting. In particular, the use of pickup trucks. As for this one…it was filled to capacity. The load was being tossed from side to side with each twist and turn of the mountain road. What was different about

CHAPTER 15: It's Dangerous. But I Went Anyway

this load though, it was full of people. Standing room only. I had managed to get one of the remaining spots. On the outside rear bumper. It was hang on or fall off.

These open air pickup truck "taxis" are an everyday form of transport. Back home, we'd be locked up for having just one person in the back. But here it's the norm. Not just one, but so many crammed in the rear of the vehicle it bottoms out over every hump. But oblivious to it all, or the simple wooden plank for those who can sit, people are smiling and casually chatting. Mums with babies, kids and even the likes of a young guy in a black suit and vest on his way home from his bank job.

This particular day, I was with this great bunch of young people. Beneficiaries of the Forma Foundation. An organisation that funds high school education for a group of highly motivated young teenagers from poor backgrounds. The foundation also funds some of these students to the USA for intensive English training. As well, they provide support to gain university scholarships in the USA. In return, they help educate younger children in their community. With the prevalence of junk food, the foundation also provides hundreds of daily nutritional snacks to nearby schools. The success of this foundation is very much the result of the passion of its founders, Candelaria and Gregorio, both from poor backgrounds themselves. From selling pencils on the street and vegetables in the market from as young as 5 years old, they have not only established a thriving Spanish school business, but use much of the proceeds to fund their worthwhile foundation.

The kids I met are a delight. You can marvel at the volcanoes. Tour the beautiful lake. Or enjoy the buzz of the markets. For me, spending some time helping these kids in just a small way with their English, was even more of a highlight.

They say it's dangerous here. But take a look at what you'd miss out on.

Chapter 16

TERRORISTS. REALLY?

It's hard to imagine that just over twenty years ago Guatemala was at war with itself. The country's army, its government and the wealthy elite warring against its own people. Huge parts of the population were razed. They were massacred, their lands, crops, belongings, houses, clothes all destroyed. Up to 45,000 civilians "disappeared" during the 36-year conflict. An estimated 200,000 were killed. A 1983 documentary film, "When The Mountains Tremble" provides an excellent description of this war between the Guatemalan Military and the Mayan Indigenous population of Guatemala. The film was used as forensic evidence in the Guatemalan court for crimes against humanity. The film centres on the experiences of Nobel Prize winner Rigoberta Menchú, a Quiché indigenous woman. She won the Nobel Peace Prize in 1992.

Growing up in that period, on the other side of the world, we heard one side of the conflict. Our government's view. The other side, the baddies. The terrorists. However, talking to the indigenous people about this war, you get a very different understanding of the conflict. Basically, the indigenous and the poor were being, to be blunt, screwed by the wealthy. The rich got richer, the poor got poorer. The government supported the wealthy. Along with USA influence. This conflict was also compounded by the west's paranoia of socialism and therefore communism, at the time.

Gaining an understanding of this conflict from the other side raises a fundamental point. At least to me anyway. When you hear the term terrorist from your government, don't necessarily believe what you are told. It may take fifty or so years for the real reason to surface. Ask the question, what has driven these people to be in conflict. In the case of this war, it started as a simple protest against a huge inequity against workers. What would any of us do in that situation if our genuine voices were continually ignored? Unfortunately, it inevitably leads to conflict and war. And typically, atrocities that occur on both sides.

Undoubtedly, when your country has a long history of being at war with itself, there is going to be a residual element of ongoing danger. I was advised that Guatemala, as with its immediate neighbouring Central American countries, were too dangerous. It was suggested to keep away.

But as a tourist, the reality is far different than this generalised level of fear. What is revealed are a number of well worn tourist destinations that take you from one amazing experience to another. And with the most organised and modern network of buses that crisscross the country and between countries. The key point is, you are not travelling alone. However, I did learn later, there is still evidence of high risk. Several weeks after I was there, a news item reported a tourist bus, including a young Australian couple, was ambushed and held up by bandits shooting at the bus. The passengers were tied up and robbed of their valuable possessions. Scary indeed. Would I travel there again? Yes. But maybe not at night.

To not venture into a place like Guatemala would be to miss so many memorable highlights. The inspiring people you meet, living amongst a community where women and men wear their traditional, intricately hand-woven clothes. Where in each town around the lake, the women dress in a colour unique to their town. Some blue. Others red. The buzz of riding on the back of a pickup truck taxi alongside the smiling and friendly people of this Mayan community that dates back thousands of years. To see the ruins of this ancient indigenous Mayan civilization that spread from Honduras, across to Tikal (Flores) in Guatemala, to Mexico.

Witnessing girls as young as maybe seven carrying buckets of sand on their heads. Their slightly older brothers hunched over hauling bags of sand on their backs strapped around their head, carting their loads up steep steps. As these Mayan people have done for thousands of years.

To be inspired by one of the young teenagers from such a background, who in my little English tuition session, said with confidence before we left, he wants to work in robotics. I have no doubt he will. It may be a road less travelled, but it's a road rich in beauty, experience and human inspiration

There is however, another serious hazard to travellers. Many tourists may not be familiar with the name, but it's one of the serious hazards all the same. The dreaded AFC Syndrome. There are different strains of it throughout many parts of the world. It can literally run you down and completely ruin your vacation. I could sense I was in danger of becoming susceptible to the local strain of this syndrome. Characteristically, it sneaks up on you without you being aware. Then before you know it, you're another victim. I chose to proceed with caution.

The best solution I felt was to get off the mainland. Like an island in the Caribbean, off the coast of Belize. Belize is the last of the Central America countries before Mexico. I've always had a curiosity about Belize. That was after I got cleaned up of a few grand some many years ago. It was one of those too good to be true investments. It sure was. Turned out it was a Ponzi scheme run by some fraudulent character residing in Belize. It would be nice, I thought, to see how my contribution had helped to fund his lifestyle. Belize, a country of only 300,000 is the most expensive of the Central American countries. Maybe that's because the native language is uniquely English.

They also have another claim to fame. Belize has the third highest national murder rate in the world. I was not out to take unnecessary risk. I assumed the weapon of choice for those contributing to this national acclaim is guns. As such I wanted to make sure I avoided the likelihood of any cross fire that may find itself contributing to the next statistic. As such, I adopted a defensive precautionary approach. I'd learnt this strategy from the movies. Darting from pillar to pillar, crouching behind corners of each building, a quick visual check before dashing to the next position. I found it took longer than everyone else to move around the city. It was also very tiring. Particularly with a full backpack. So I was pleased to get out of the city. I chose to spend the rest of my two day Belize experience in the country's popular Caye Caulker Island. It's a pleasant forty minute ferry ride from the city.

CHAPTER 16: Terrorists. Really?

I had only just arrived on the island. The reality of the well established tourist trails navigating backpackers throughout central America, became even more evident. Two groups of people I had travelled with a month or two ago, each in different countries of Central America, I now met up with again, wandering down the island's main street.

One of the main attractions on the island is snorkelling. The snorkelling was great. But what I wasn't so keen on was the large abundance of stingrays that surrounded us. Maybe it's the fresh memories of Steve Irwin's final encounter, but I was happy to keep my distance. There was one other hazard I was not prepared for. That is, dodging everyone else's selfie stick mounted GoPro. I was the standout. I was the only one that didn't have one. So last year, I thought of myself. I always thought I was pretty tech savvy. Like being able to shoot live video back home. Such as a live video commentary back to my 84 year old mother while weaving in and around busy city streets in a tuk tuk.

Actually, we don't call her cyber granny for no reason. She's as hooked up as the best of us. Come to think of it, she could probably do with a selfie stick GoPro for her next cruise. What a hoot. I can just see it. There'd be Great Granny wallowing in the pool with all the other oldies, cocktail in one hand and her selfie stick GoPro in the other.

Having to leave the stingrays and the thought of mother and her GoPro selfie stick behind, it was time to leave the island and head back to the mainland. Tulum in Mexico is a pleasant afternoon bus ride further north across the border. With a street lined with restaurants cafes and bars, there's a noticeably higher level of tourism sophistication here, than its southern country cousins.

But it was now time to face my fears. The potential AFC Syndrome. AFC Syndrome originates in England. There's been well documented case studies of AFC, particularly for first time travellers to England. You've no doubt experienced it yourself if you've toured there. That's right, "Another F#@#%@% Castle." A strain of the syndrome known as AFT occurs in South East Asia due to similar levels of high exposure to temples. Here in Central America, the AFR strain is widespread.

But first, can you answer this one question for me please? Am I the only one that had never heard of the Mayan civilisation? Or was I nodding off again during that part of my ancient history school lessons? I don't know how I could have missed this piece of ancient history, as there's ancient Mayan ruins all over the place here. Of course, the danger is it means being susceptible to the local strain of the AFR Syndrome. The Ruins of Tulum, an enjoyable twenty minute bicycle ride from town, is one of these sites. Fortunately, this one is right on the coast. With the beautiful Caribbean coast line, if I was a Mayan back then, I would definitely have chosen to live here.

Having fortunately avoided the AFR Syndrome, venturing further north along the Mexican coast reveals even further increased tourism development. The main street of Playa del Carmen. It's like a Gold Coast strip offering all the usual tourism razzamatazz of merchandise and services shopping. The beach front below is amass with high end condos and private hotels. Clearly not for backpackers. As soon as I stepped over the line in the sand, little men in white outfits topped off with official looking shoulder lapels, a shiny name badge and their very own

CHAPTER 16: Terrorists. Really?

walkie talkie, were there to quickly remind me I had encroached their space one step too far! Mmmm.

Cancun, top of the Caribbean coastal strip is a favourite for many North Americans. I can see why. Beautiful beaches. Delightful weather and great food. A perfect winter getaway. I'm not sure if there's a syndrome for excessive exposure to lovely sand, beach and sun. I expect not.

Travel back in time and experience a taste of the Caribbean coast.

Chapter 17

CUBA. A PRODUCT OF TWO EXTREMES?

Interesting parallels with Guatemala, Cuba was another case of the rich get richer, the poor get poorer. Extreme capitalism. Suddenly replaced by revolutionary Fidel Castro's brand of socialism. History again now shines a different light from that which our governments were shining at places like Cuba back then. Big bad Fidel was the image portrayed back in the sixties. Fast forward to current times and there's widespread support for what Castro did against the huge disparity of extreme capitalism that created a huge social chasm.

Is Cuba today a product of two extremes? Trapped in an economic time warp for half a century. Where all the monuments of capitalism, hotels, the businesses and the numerous grand homes, were seized by the state.

I didn't realise I was witnessing that wealth. I had just arrived in Havana. The taxi was making its way to my homestay, known locally as a Casa Particular. The taxi driver remarked how I was staying in the upmarket part of town. I thought I had misunderstood him. It certainly didn't look upmarket to me. The streets had a distinct run down, unkept appearance. But I was soon to realise he was right. Look beyond the derelict, unkept buildings and a past era of astonishing wealth is revealed. Grand mansions that once shone with wealth, lined one after another along the leafy streets. These buildings, unless taken over as embassies, are now left in decaying ruins. Central to this area of historic wealth is even a Fifth Avenue, providing a parallel to the wealth back in New York.

To me, Cuba's history is an example highlighting the need for a balanced mix of socialism with capitalism. Regardless, the result today is that Cuba is a unique country tourists can't get enough of. A country with the sparse to the plentiful. The beauty to the ugly. The grandiose to the neglected. The gleaming old convertible classics to the rattly old bone shakers. Where rural settings make you swear you're in the set of an old western movie with more men on horses and horse drawn carts than vehicles. Where you pinch yourself to check what year it is as you see fifty year old Chevrolets or Oldsmobiles charging along the highway. But it's as if the Cuban people said, "so what." They may have been shunned by western world politics with decades of trade embargoes. But they were free. Free to create a vibrant culture filled with their resourcefulness and artistic talent.

Where not only colourful art fills the streets, but music. In places you would not expect. Like the History Museum in

Cuba, a living museum of the old filled with a vibrant culture of people and arts.

CHAPTER 17: Cuba. A Product of Two Extremes?

Trinidad. There was a somewhat out of place grand piano in the corner of the museum. "Don't Touch" the sign said. But suddenly, the normally staid and sterile walls were echoing the sound of beautiful music. Now seated at the piano was a young Cuban girl. Her fingers eloquently dancing across the keys. Each touch filling the building with music as it overflowed onto the street. Leidiana is only fourteen. She's only been playing for five years. Has had no formal training. And plays completely by ear. No music. Maybe one day there'll be much grander walls echoing the sound of an appreciative applause to this young girl's talent. But such ability is normal in Cuba, I was told.

Outside in the town square, the sun was yet to descend. But already the heart of the city was pulsating to the beat of live music. The heat of the day slowly making way for another warm balmy night. The clip clopping of horses and their carts on the cobblestone road beginning to subside. The uneven roads instead filling with people moving purposely towards the town square's swelling crowd. Swaying to the rhythm. Chatting. Absorbing the buzz. Cerveza beers quenching thirsts. Or one of the many popular Cuban rum cocktails. The ten piece music group enthralling the crowd. Dancing spontaneously erupting throughout the crowd. And as if to ensure the experience doesn't end there, just a step outside the square, numerous restaurants each waiting to embrace you with their own live musical experience. Is Trinidad, Cuba, the soul of Latino Americano music? Or just a tourist stage? Either way, it's well and truly like no other.

There's another fantastic advantage Cuba offers. A health benefit. The longer you stay, the longer you detox. An internet detox, that is. No internet. You can get it. It's just a matter of finding it. It's like playing a game of treasure hunt…Cuban style. The way you play the game is to look for urban wifi clues. These are the wifi hotspots sparsely located around the city. The way to identify them is to look for a collection of small idle groups of people with mobile phone in hand. They'll be squatting under a tree, on a park bench or standing peering towards a pole. In some countries you'd assume this stance to represent some type of God worship. But here, on closer inspection you can see it's the closest you can get to the wifi antenna mounted up a pole. The signal's stronger. That's the first part of the challenge. The next part is you need to find the hawkers. They sell the wifi login cards. Three cuc's ($3) for an hour. Most times these guys will spot you before you find them. The dilemma is when you finally find a wifi hotspot, but no hawker to buy a ticket. It's all part of the fun of playing Cuban internet treasure hunt.

Cuba. It's what tourists can't get enough of.

Chapter 18

OUR FASCINATION WITH OLD STUFF

It felt just like back home. A delightful city environment. And after two weeks in Cuba, supermarkets actually full of stock. This is popular Miraflores in Lima, Peru. Offering a vast choice of restaurants to enjoy what Peru is famous for…food. Plus, lovely parks, surrounds and beach front parks. Then there's the city centre with its grand colonial buildings. Noticeably, what stands out are the brightly painted buildings. Apparently, that's to make up for the high percentage of grey skied days.

The grey skies unfortunately don't provide much rain it seems. The city receives next to no annual rainfall (9mm). In fact, Lima is the world's second largest city located on a desert, after Cairo. It's main water source is the River Rimac. You'd wanna love that river.

The city of ten million is not all pristine. Move outside the popular tourist destinations and you find the slums where seventy percent of the city live. Cross over the bridge from the bustling tourist centric city centre, we were told it is not advised to go. Too dangerous. Not quite like home, yet within the tourist areas, what a lovely city.

Next destination Machu Picchu. Fortunately, there's the popular Peru Hop On Off bus. A great service set up by a couple of Irish guys a few years ago. Instead of flying, the hop on bus takes you to a range of interesting destinations south of Peru. All a bit touristy. But then again, I'm not Christopher Columbus. Typically, a six day trip…stop off for a few hours, or stay a few days at each place…you decide. Takes in some fantastic sites like Ballestas Islands. Referred to as the young cousin of Galapagos Islands with sea lions and bountiful numbers of bird life (and a fertiliser side industry from all the bird poop). My favourite stop off, Huacachinero. It's where the sand buggy and sand boarding tours, with their crazy drivers, take you for a heart stopping, back breaking tour through the massive sand hills surrounding this very picturesque desert oasis town. Chincha, home to the secret slave tunnels. The mysterious Nazca lines. Colca Canyon, twice as deep as the Grand Canyon. And one of the features of the tour, Lake Titicaca the world's highest navigable lake with man-made floating islands.

Sand Buggying in Huacachinero. Absolutely crazy. But what fun!

But one of the highlights of travel are the ones that go beyond the tourist icons of mountains and grand buildings. If you were having a family fiesta similar to a wedding and a bunch of five vagabond foreigners were peering through the gated door curious about the local culture going on inside, would you invite them in? In Puno on Lake Titicaca in Peru, that's what they did. The

CHAPTER 18: Our Fascination with Old Stuff

Bulgarian, the Cyprus couple, the Scot and me, the Aussie. Treated to whiskey, beer, dancing. What a welcoming treat of Peruvian hospitality. Unfortunately, we couldn't party through the night till 7am as our welcoming host had suggested. We had to leave to catch our overnight bus. Thank you, Puno, for one of those special golden moments of travel.

Good old fashioned hospitality is not the only standout treat to experience in Peru. It's their old stuff. What is it that so fascinates us about old stuff? Antique shops thrive to support our fix to fill our houses with old stuff. Stuff we don't even use. Only to look at and spend time dusting. Old vintage cars that enthusiasts spend meticulous hours restoring to every original detail. We collect stamps, old books we never read again, childhood dolls and toys we never touch again.

You name it, if it's old there'll be someone collecting enough of it to make a museum of it. And what we can't collect, we'll go out of our way to see. Like the million people each year who visit Machu Picchu in Peru. We'll travel from across the globe. By plane, bus, train and finally by foot, each getting us that one step closer to our long held dream to step back into a page of our ancient past. In our quest to embrace the old, we then form part of a huge tourist factory. A mega dollar machine where we are shuffled and directed from one part of the human tourist machine to the next.

It's a small price we pay though, for the experience. Maybe it's our inherent desire to satisfy our endless curiosity about ourselves. But when it comes to Machu Picchu, you gotta feel sorry for the poor ol' Incas. They decide to build this city up in the mountains. It takes about two and a half thousand men over sixty to seventy years to build the place. And it's no mean feat. Massive stones of twenty tons intricately carved and positioned into place. But where you feel for them, after that mind boggling effort to build the place, they abandon it. That's after living there for only thirty five years. Those Spanish again.

They'd taken over the rest of the continent. The Incas weren't going to let the Spanish have this prize little spot. To destroy their temples as they commonly did in favour of complying with the conquerors religious demands. So, they took off. To the likes of the Amazon. Trouble is they never came back. And the Spanish thankfully never found it. Not until close to four hundred years later in 1911 when an American historian stumbled across it. The rest is now history, so to speak.

Machu Picchu. If I had a bucket list, it would have been on the list.

If I had a bucket list, Machu Picchu would have been on it. And it certainly didn't disappoint. Just the stunning backdrop alone with its impressive mountains, snow-capped peaks in the background and the gushing river below. All this topped up with a spread of wispy clouds to finish off this magical landscape setting.

While the roofs may have succumbed to the odd storm over the centuries, the building structures primarily remain. There's no question the Incas left us a gift. A gift for us to not only admire their stunning location, but to feed our curiosity. To have us ponder and debate what our predecessor's lives were like. And as we post our selfies online for all to see, maybe we've gained at least one thing from all this old stuff. The comfort of making us

CHAPTER 18: Our Fascination with Old Stuff

feel, that maybe our lives in the now are really so much better.

But there's one little prized find that neither the Incas, nor the Spanish or any lot before them found. Except in historical terms, just a few of us over the last couple of years have witnessed. That's because for all this time it's remained hidden. Until just recently. It's one of the benefits of climate change. What until now has been covered in snow has now revealed a newly discovered feature that is proving a very popular tourist destination. Set in magnificent scenery, the challenge of getting there makes it all the more rewarding.

It's an early morning departure from Cusco for the three hour bus ride to the site. Then a three hour trek to the mountain. It makes for a long and tiring day. But what climate change has revealed is now known as Rainbow Mountain. It's probably a fair criticism the local tour companies have been a bit creative on their brochures with the intensity of the rainbow colours. But, yes, I'm sure with the sun in the right place it could possibly get close to resembling the colours of a rainbow.

At the same height as Mt Everest base camp, the lack of oxygen and the threat of altitude sickness adds to the challenge. The overall trek is a steady climb. However, the last stage of the trek really reveals the effects of altitude. It's a very slow zimmer frame like one step at a time motion. There's plenty of horses for hire to make it easier. But it's doable. Especially on the way back

Global Warming reveals amazing discovery. But did we find the pot of gold?

when you can actually get a spring in your step descending down the mountain.

All rainbows have a pot of gold at the end. Right? Someone must have beaten us to it though. Nonetheless, we still must have been lucky. According to later reports, if the conditions are wet, the experience of this trek is not pleasant at all and widely suggested it's not recommended. I can understand why. The infrastructure of the track to get there would be a huge mud fest challenge. It's not quite up to Machu Picchu tourism standard. But that's also the attraction.

Despite not finding the pot of gold, the search for hidden treasure continues as the bus travels further up Peru's north coast. It's an all nighter bus. There's nothing to see. On day break you can see why. Just large tracts of desert. At least in our deserts down under we throw in a few rocks, trees and dry river beds here and there. By contrast here, there's sand hill after sand hill. At least until you get further north, nudging closer to the equator.

There is water. You just have to find it. While it looks dry and barren, there's obviously water there. That's because there was this ancient Chimor empire who loved playing with mud. They were good at it. So good they built cities with it that can still be seen today. One city, Chan Chan (meaning Sun-Sun…they must have had a stuttering problem back then), an overnight bus trip north of Lima, had an estimated population of around 60,000.

But here's where it gets interesting. This Chimu lot predated the Incas. So along came the Incas. Now just when I was feeling sorry for them at the hands of the Spanish. Turns out they're not much better. They liked what the Chimas had. Knocked them off

CHAPTER 18: Our Fascination with Old Stuff

and took over their city. Had no interest in their gold. Of course, not that it was safe for too long. Not until the salivating Spanish set their eyes on it after they knocked off the Incas.

There's a moral to this story from history. Thou shalt feel free to covet thy neighbour's property, because in a few hundred years there's a good chance you'll be famous with tourists crawling over each other to view the remnants of your prized haul.

Invasions have been part of this region's history for centuries. But it's very curious as to why Latin America, with all its magnificent natural beauty and vast resources, has been left so far behind the rest of the developed world economically.

It all started with the Spanish. And sadly, it hasn't stopped to this day. Historians consider the continent's current struggles a result of five centuries of pillage and plundering by foreign invaders. The Spanish and their conquistadors started by pillaging the massive lodes of silver and gold. Next were the Portuguese taking aim at Brazil's rich resources. The resources of the continent were seen as seemingly never-ending.

Next was the impact of sugar. This was a commodity seen by the world market with similar value to gold or silver. Unfortunately, as with the gold and silver before it, this resource, along with bananas, coffee, cacao, nitrates, cotton, rubber and petroleum were also plundered by foreign interests. Foreign powers took the riches. The poorer, more dependent countries were left with exhausted soil. Impoverished workers barely survived on the lowly wages or the food they worked for.

The English also got into the act. They set up agreements with Portugal and Spain. They took the larger proportion of the profits leaving the poorer Latin American countries in even worse conditions. Left relying on just their natural resources, they were not able to develop any industrial infrastructure.

As the centuries went by, Latin American dictators emerged. They formed self-serving agreements with the foreign interests. The dictator's motives were predominantly to increase their own profits and positions of power. The dictators, by aiding the continued plunder and abuse of their land and people, caused as much damage to their own countries as did the foreign invaders. The pillage and abuse of Latin America continues. To this day, it is argued the United States is considered the new conquistador. That is by furthering the tradition of the Europeans through agreements with Latin American countries that favour them in tariffs, taxes and profits.

Moving around the countries of Latin America, there's one word that keeps coming up. Corruption. Every country has it. It just seems it's more embedded in the culture here.

An excellent book, "Open Veins of Latin America: Five Centuries of the Pillage of a Continent", by well respected author, Eduardo Galeano, offers a detailed account on this part of Latin America's sad history.

Join me as we tour Peru. From south to north. Experience all its natural wonders just waiting for you to enjoy.

Chapter 19

EACH DAY, A NEW SURPRISE

You could call it the cycle of life. Remember the times as a young, single person. Life is very flexible. If you decide to do something, you do it. A partner joins you. Decisions are now subject to consensus or negotiation. First child arrives. Any activity such as a day out requires measured pre-planning. Spare nappies, clothes, prams, etc, etc. Second child, further planning required. Ramp up the family to include three kids, you are now at a military level of strategic planning. That's before you even step out the door. If in fact you consider it worthwhile. As the kids leave home it's a gradual step back to greater flexibility. Find yourself single again, you're back to the flexibility of a teenager.

And so it was with this journey. Youthful style flexibility. With lots of surprises. When several people say a destination has been one of their highlights, it's worth taking notice of. It also adds a touch of adventure. Like for example these next two destinations…

I was heading for a trip into the Amazon Jungle. "I don't want to scare you", I was told. The bus was nearing the end of our seven hour journey from Quito, the capital city of Ecuador in South America. "Don't go out alone. And when you get to the bus station, go straight to a taxi". He was a military guy returning to duty on the nearby Colombian border. "Terrorists," he had explained in our earlier chat on the journey. "Cross the border, we shoot them."

Despite his day job, he seemed a likeable sort of guy. So, in a calm but focused acceptance of this seemingly qualified advice, on arrival at the bus terminal I headed straight to the first exit. There was one problem. In my haste, I had taken a side exit. I suddenly found myself on an isolated, dark street. Not what I had expected. Nor the situation you want in any city, let alone one with this reputation. Not a taxi in sight. Fortunately, though, one wasn't far away.

Lago Agrio is a sort of a gateway last point of civilization before the Amazon. I'd heard similar warnings about this town. I therefore accepted that an evening walk, particularly at night, was clearly not an option. What supported this reputation was when I enquired where to eat. Without hesitation, the hotel manager turned up to drive me to a restaurant. "So, this place is pretty dangerous", I said with an air of informed certainty.

Turns out the opinion of those in the local tourism and hospitality industry is quite a contrast. But go back about ten years they agree, it was anything but safe. That all came to an end, the story goes, when guerrilla fighters from across the Colombian border decided to take the law into their own hands. Anyone outside of an imposed curfew was shot. No questions asked. It took a week of "cleaning up" apparently, and the town has never looked back!!

It's a strange trait of human nature. On one hand we go to extraordinary lengths to offer compassion and help to our fellow human beings. We create social communities that support each

CHAPTER 19: Each Day, A New Surprise

other. Yet on the other hand we have this extreme, destructive capacity to seek and destroy each other.

Nowhere else could that be so evident as in nature. Particularly the Amazon jungle. Step into this truly amazing yet mysterious part of our planet and discover some of the most incredible interconnected forces of nature. An amazingly intricate web of indescribable intelligence between so many diverse facets of nature, whether trees, animals, bugs, insects, bacteria, fungi, etc. Where survival is eat or be eaten. Yet at the same time there's an enormous display of cooperation between the different elements of nature.

Eat or be Eaten. A journey into the Amazon jungle.

Now I'll admit I'm not normally a bird watching, tree hugging sort of bloke. But to spend several days deep in the Amazon with one of the local indigenous people was impressive. Where he not only spots the tiniest creature a mile off but rattles off the name of every variety. And to have explained so many examples of how nature works together to protect against nature's aggressors.

Like my favourite, the woodpecker. He doesn't make the hole for his nest. He just starts it. He comes back later after fungi has taken over to enlarge the hole, formed in such a way to keep aggressors from the young'uns. And when woody wood pecker has finished nesting, he hands it over to the owl. By then a bigger hole. Who would have guessed!

And as well to hear how other indigenous locals describe their home as not just a jungle of trees but as a living spirit of energy, almost people like, as one explained. But more so to gain just a small appreciation of the amazing world we live in. And none more so incredible than the Amazon jungle.

But one question still remained. Do the likes of trees have their own form of intelligence or are they each so incredibly genetically wired to be able to react and respond to all the many unpredictable forces of nature?

From the jungle to the middle of the Pacific. This was another case of teenage level flexibility. A decision on the fly. Many people had said a trip to this destination was a must. So, one morning, I happened to wake at 5:30am. I thought, let's go. Packed the backpack. Caught a taxi to the airport. Booked a flight and by that afternoon was on an island in the middle of the Pacific Ocean. A thousand kilometres off the Ecuadorian coast. It wasn't what I had expected. In fact, on some parts of the island, I doubt the moon would be this rugged. It's certainly not the image you associate with a tropical island.

We'd trekked up to the main volcano on the island. It's the second largest in the world measuring ten kilometres across. The recent eruption just over ten years ago had left a blackened charred plateau across the inside of this massive crater. The previous eruption was not so gentle. It spilled over the huge crater spewing lava far down to the sea. What it left behind was a hostile landscape. The only sign of life amongst the charred layers of jagged and rugged volcanic black rocks are the scattered and incredibly hardy cactus bush. Their thorny prickles as if to guard against any intrusion to their unique opportunity for life.

For the people who live on islands such as Isabela Island, I guess they have the volcanoes to thank for creating their home. But it comes at a price. That jagged volcanic rock is literally their backyard between each house.

CHAPTER 19: Each Day, A New Surprise

But the contrast to the coast couldn't be more dramatic. Pristine white, sandy beaches. And an incredible array of wildlife. It's what makes the Galapagos islands so unique. Swimming with giant sea turtles seemingly oblivious to your presence can only be described as an amazing experience. Or walking amongst the huge tortoises that live up to 120 years. The prehistoric looking iguanas that look like a mini version of their dinosaur ancestors. Or the docile layabout sea lions that quite comfortably take up residence on park benches. I guess they were there first anyway.

How could one of the most inhospitable places on earth be home to such amazing wonders of nature.

If the cost of rubbing shoulders with some of nature's greatest treasures in pristine surroundings is having a harsh moonscape in the centre of your island, it's a small price to pay. An extraordinary opportunity to experience the contrast of nature's extremes.

It's not only the many fascinating experiences of nature to be enjoyed, but so too more interesting people you meet along the way. Like chatting with a young lady and her friend I met waiting for a taxi in this small outlying village. She's using the tranquillity of the Galapagos Islands to write a book on her life-changing ordeal after being held in detention. It's not every day you get to meet one of the people you hear about on the news who has been through the ordeal of an illegal border crossing. But more so, getting caught and the experiences they endure after being thrown into detention.

It was on one of these islands, I thought I was also about to find myself in a detention centre. I had run out of money. Detention centres at least provide free accommodation and meals I thought. Until I discovered how to make my own ATM machine.

Maybe I had been taken up by too much of that teenager free spirit. Ok, so maybe you do need to do a little bit of planning. Nearly all Latin American countries only take cash. And in particular, this Galapagos Island I was on.

I had just arrived by ferry from one of the other islands. My three days of accommodation plus some tours was now paid up by cash. This left me with just a few dollars. I don't like carrying too much cash in case my wallet gets nicked, which did happen later in the trip...but that's another story for further on. "So ATM"? "Sorry sir, no ATMs on this island".

It was suddenly a very daunting feeling not even having enough money to buy a ferry ticket off the island. Let alone enough cash to live on for the next three days. I went into survival mode. With my remaining few dollars of cash, I headed off to the nearest store. Of course, cash only. I bought a packet of pasta and a can of tuna. I figured, at least I would have something to eat for a couple of meals.

Fortunately, I later discovered there was one restaurant on the island that accepted visa credit card. Putting my emergency rations aside, I ventured off to find this restaurant. The main street of this island looks more like a scene from a western movie. Big wide dusty streets with just a smattering of people. Lined up on one side of the streets are all the cafes and bars, each adding a certain rustic feel to the place. The only thing missing were the horses and the veranda posts for any bad guys in town to lean on and chew straw. It certainly wasn't high season here.

I seated myself at the restaurant. I double checked there was

CHAPTER 19: Each Day, A New Surprise

a Visa sign. I was certainly looking forward to a more deserving meal than the emergency rations I had consoled myself to accept. And here's where I set up my ATM cash machine. I sat near the payment counter. I then waited until a guest went to pay. "Excuse me are you paying by cash", I would then ask them. I then exchanged their cash for payment by card. It took a few "withdrawals", but at least I could now afford to get off the island.

There's no question. Each day is certainly a new experience. But it's these experiences that arise that make unstructured travelling so unique and exciting.

Experience a look deep into the Amazon jungle. Then across to the Galapagos Islands in the middle of the Pacific Ocean.

Chapter 20

DRUGS. I MUST HAVE BEEN LIVING UNDER A ROCK

I had her firmly in a headlock. I wasn't expecting this from my first visit to Colombia.

There's one thing you soon learn after you arrive in Cali. There are places and times when you can walk around the city. Not much different to any city, but here you need to be a lot more selective. Like there's a popular walk up to the three crosses mountain. But the advice is don't go after lunch. Beside it being too hot, you are warned it's too dangerous. Go first thing in the morning you are told. There's a good reason why. In the morning there's a strong police presence along with numerous others out for the energetic morning workout scramble up the mountain track. Any other time, you'd be doing quite a bit of looking over your shoulder. It's certainly worth the effort though. A spectacular view awaits your arrival.

But while the stigma of drug lords and gangsters persist in the minds of the global community, it's unquestionably a country in transition. And a country very proud of its moving forward. It's not that long ago tourists would avoid this country. As one young Colombian lady told me, even she and many others left their home town of Cali because it was too dangerous. She came back to visit five years ago. She was surprised how the city had changed. She's been back ever since without any regrets. The growing tourist numbers are evidence of this change. Maybe it's also because of the great climate. Interestingly two dry and two wet seasons in the one year.

The one thing Cali is famous for is salsa dancing. Claimed as the world capital of salsa. By the way, while you think of salsa as originating from Latin America, it actually originated from New York in the seventies. Regardless of who thought of it first, when in Cali do as the Cali folks do…go Salsa dancing.

It was the final part of the dance move we were being taught. It was very elegant watching the instructor. But in my case, well…I was quite a lot taller than my Colombian dance partner. With my arm wrapped around this poor lady's neck, to me it felt awkwardly more like a wrestling headlock. I'm not sure who looked worse off. Me looking awkward trying to work out how to unravel from this situation or this poor lady being near choked to death. Unfortunately, I had to leave Cali still wondering how this dance move magically unfolds.

Further north is the popular Medellin, once the world's most murderous city. And this was only back in the nineties until famous drug lord Pablo Escobar's murderous control of the city finally came to end when the kingpin was gunned down in 1993.

While the people of Colombia have had to try and forget this part of their country's past, it's quite clear they are very proud of the new progressive direction they are heading. And they clearly express their gratitude to visitors who come here. And in huge numbers.

CHAPTER 20: Drugs. I Must Have Been Living Under a Rock

Mainly young backpackers, doing the likes of the very popular daily city walking tour. In one part of the city, a level four alert area. It's here the guide advises to wear backpacks on your front!

But as in any city, being mindful of its hazards and stepping beyond the more "adventurous" part of the city, a far more positive and exciting side awaits. If you think of your own city or country, would you advise people not to visit it because of its other undesirable pockets? The same for Colombia. It has the stunning scenery you find anywhere such as in Europe, as modern infrastructure as anywhere, when compared to the rest of the world. Lovely people who create a vibrancy that explains why I have not heard of one person who has visited here that does not rave about it and want to come back. The biggest disappointment I had was not staying longer.

There are two ways to get from Colombia up to Panama. By air or sea. For those who chose by sea, it was another one of those highly talked about highlights of a trip. I chose the by sea option.

We set off on our voyage. "Another champagne"? the waiter asked with courteous attentiveness. The captain had joined our table for dinner. We were dressed in formal attire as we sat at the pristine, white tableclothed table. Silver cutlery and crystal glasses clinking as we chatted about our day of leisurely activities. By contrast, the portholes revealed a drastic contrast to the serenity we were enjoying inside our cruise ship. A raging storm had come from nowhere as the rain pelted against the glass. I was day dreaming of course.

It was bucketing down with rain, though. And yes, I was in a boat. But there were no portholes. And this boat had no white tableclothed tables and served no champagne. The captain was

One of the trip highlights – crossing from Colombia to Panama by an open boat.

steering the boat and was getting as drenched as the rest of us. We were making our way from Colombia to Panama along the coast. It was a long, open boat with a couple of outboards on the back and just a sun canopy. As we were being pelted with rain, I looked around to the other passengers to see how they were weathering the storm. There was one poor guy taking the full force of a water like jet streaming off the canopy roof. There were a couple of young Aussie girls who took an innovative approach. They put on their snorkel masks. As the rain pelted through the boat as if oblivious to the roof, I pulled the hood of my poncho firmly over my face. I wondered what it would be like to be instead in that mental picture I'd painted of that cruise ship.

Bugger that, I thought as I smirked to myself. I was on an adventure. There was no comparison. However, I was soon to realise I must have spent my life living under a rock. What I experienced would change my view on one of society's biggest issues. Drugs.

I was one of twenty one doing the crossing by boat, the others nearly all young Aussies with a sprinkling of a few other nationalities. Nice group of young people. I was definitely the old man of the trip however. The trip was over four days with three nights staying on a different island of the San Blas Island archipelago. Two of the island visits are spent staying in the native villages of the Kuna people. How they got there…well it's those Spanish again who back in the 1500's drove them off the mainland.

The first challenge of the trip was the border crossing. We

CHAPTER 20: Drugs. I Must Have Been Living Under a Rock

were warned not to take drugs across the border, unless we wanted to spend the next ten years in a Colombian gaol. So here we are all lined up at the border. We were required to open our backpacks and lay them in a row on the ground. Meanwhile the local customs officer was desperately trying to restrain his sniffer dog. It's as if his dog was already onto something. Not that I had any reason for concern, but just to make sure, I will admit before I left the dormitory that morning, I did double check the contents of my backpack.

Now I don't know much about drugs, or how far cocaine scent wafts, but as another precaution, I did discreetly move my backpack right to the end of the row. As I mentioned, I had no reason to be concerned, but I can assure you the heart was pumping overtime as that dog sniffed across each bag. We were all given the ok. "Phew", I thought to myself. Along with quite a few other relieved faces too, I might add.

The last island we had almost to ourselves. If you think of your typical idyllic tropical castaway island, the San Blas Islands couldn't fit that description any better. Pristine white sand, palm trees, crystal clear water with perfect temperature. The only hazard is the possibility of a falling coconut. A hut with a room full of hammocks provided the beds for the night. But it was party night.

Well, there was no shortage of cocaine. Delivered by a local islander. And no shortage of participants. Except for one. Despite numerous offers. Don't get me wrong, I love a good party. I was happy to contend with a few beers and the odd swig out of the flagon of rum as it was passed around. I've never taken drugs and I wasn't about to start that night.

But what stood out to me, here was a cross section of a good bunch of young people. But their attitude and experience to drugs was completely foreign to me. I had several discussions with them about this, as well as other people I met along the way. The bottom line is, if you want any illicit drug, they all say it's dead set easy to get. If they choose not to, they don't take drugs. Simple as that. The bottom line is, young people are already making choices.

So as was once the case with alcohol, why bother with prohibition? My question is, wouldn't it be better to take control of this market? Thereby taking the money away from the crime related drug lords, thereby removing the drug traffickers and therefore the pressure to get people involved with drugs. Plus, by legalising it, what we spend on fighting drugs, could be used to educate people on the use of drugs. They're already making that choice. Why not help them make a more informed choice?

I was first exposed to the extent of this drug culture at a book launch back in Nicaragua. The book was written by a young North American traveller about his globetrotting experience. He spoke openly of his experience with drugs. He was talking about it like we talk about selecting a drink from a bar. I remember looking across at a couple, quite older than myself. As we listened to this young person's account, I was curious to observe their reaction. Soon after, they left. I assumed out of total unacceptance. Unless, because it was getting late!?

Curious, I raised this subject to discuss with a number of other young people I met along the way. One such person, a funny and charming English guy (his description – it was a tongue in cheek condition he made with me to use his quote...unless he

CHAPTER 20: Drugs. I Must Have Been Living Under a Rock

was serious?!!) Jokes aside, to me, he made a staggering comment. He took this line of thinking even further. He said the choice of his closest friends would depend on if they had experienced a certain hallucinogenic drug. Purely for the reason that it exposed them to a deeper level of thinking.

Among the Indigenous peoples of the Amazon basin, hallucinogenic preparations, such as ayahuasca, have been long used as a traditional spiritual medicine in ceremonies. It is used largely as a treasured sacrament. Participants report spiritual revelations regarding their purpose on earth, the true nature of the universe and a deeper insight into how to be the best person they possibly can.

Drugs unquestionably continue as one of our biggest threats to society. Maybe we need to really face hard facts and review our attitude and ignorance of drugs. Perhaps then we can offer our younger generation a more open and trusted source to better equip them to make more informed choices.

Meanwhile back on the island, the starlit night glistening a reflection over the water created a memorable night. In more ways than one. Around the flickering fire, the party continued to sway. There were the odd high fives. The occasional, "You're a legend, mate" (not sure if that was because they had the equivalent to their old man there). And the odd questions that came up like "what was it like in your day"?! I wondered if and when such changes in attitude to the world of drugs would ever happen. For our generation, somehow, I can't see it happening anytime soon. For me, well I've certainly managed to get plenty of highs out of just liv'n life.

Drugs or no drugs, you'll love Colombia and the San Blas Islands.

Chapter 21

CLIMATE CHANGE, WHO CARES?

It was every person's dream. It wasn't just the generously appointed home, but the lush natural beauty of the garden setting. An enviable touch of paradise. Centrepiece a waterfall. With crystal clear water tumbling over a backdrop of rocks, making its way down to a well-stocked fishpond below. The owner was a generous man. He demanded little. He'd invited his guests to make use of his property for the year. At absolutely no cost.

But what happened by the end of that twelve months would shock you. As if disrespecting their landlord's generosity, what was once a pristine estate had now neglectfully deteriorated. More fish were now floating than swimming. The air was tainted with smouldering remains of waste. Rubbish littered all corners of the property. Sounds like one of those tenants from hell stories you see on TV. And what's this got to do with this trip I hear you ask?

It was one of those long fifteen hour flights across the globe. Glancing through the window, the majesty of that huge wing carrying us thirty thousand feet up caught my attention. I reflected further on the natural majesty of the world below. The sheer beauty. Some of which I had just experienced. The magic of the earth that endlessly produces to perpetually sustain life.

But like that fable above, are we all not like those tenants? The reality is, in close to a hundred years not one of us will be here any longer. Our tenancy will be up. We will have then handed it over to the next tenants. Our next generations.

But what state will we have left it in? Will our legacy be one we'd proudly leave to our next generations? Now don't get me wrong. I don't see myself as some tree hugging environmentalist. In fact, I'll admit I'm even a sceptic when it comes to human caused climate change. The reality is, you don't have to be a rocket scientist or an environmental expert to see what's happening.

How much we are literally defecating in our own global backyard. Air pollution, contamination of our waterways, and most visible of all, our massive waste, the endless plastic our bloated consumerism generates. Developing countries like Latin America and Asia for example, are stunningly beautiful. But regardless, it seems there is an ingrained culture that accepts to simply throw stuff at it. Their roads and highways are glaring examples. In some areas, it's indescribable.

I was travelling through Honduras in Central America. We'd stopped to the side of this mountain road. The scenery with the far-reaching mountain ranges that surrounded us would have been breathtaking. But what actually took your breath away was the extraordinarily huge amount of rubbish that littered all the way along the stretches of the highway.

My last day in Panama. A car is stopped at the lights. The

CHAPTER 21: CLIMATE CHANGE, WHO CARES?

door opens. Out drops a plastic bag of rubbish onto the street. A motorbike rider in Cambodia finishes his drink. Spontaneously he ditches the disposable plastic cup to the side of the road. In both cases the growing piles of scattered rubbish clearly says it's the norm.

But before we all smugly shake our heads in aloof disgust, it wasn't that long ago we were no different. The difference now is, just like those tenants, we share the problem. It's where this leg of the journey clearly brought the message home.

I had time for one more movie. I'll admit my final choice wasn't the type of film I felt bothered to watch. But I did anyway. I'm glad I did. "A Plastic Ocean". An excellent documentary. It makes a critical point. We have a global problem. We and our families and those that follow us are now and will continue to be affected. I urge you to watch it. What happens on one side of the world is impacting what we eat and our health, on the other side of the globe.

In Thailand and Cambodia for example, what are otherwise pristine beaches, are now becoming awash with plastic waste of every imaginable consumer item. Washed up from the sea. For resort owners, it's now a daily task to clear the waste washed up overnight. Our crazy love affair of plastic drink bottles has grown exponentially. So much so you now see pallets of these bottles stacked outside shops because there's not enough room inside the supermarket. But where is it likely to end up? Much of it eventually washed down from the land, into the river and out to sea. Soon at a pristine beach near you.

On arriving in Singapore, I couldn't help but notice, by comparison, the amazing difference as to how litter free this city is. It may be one of the cleanest cities in the world, my driver explained, but he was convinced their imported food from neighbouring countries were the cause of his various health ailments.

This documentary on plastic waste makes that exact point. We share the problem globally. It focuses on our insidious amount of waste. In particular, plastic. It reminds me of when I was growing up in Australia. We had exactly the same cultural mentality of what you see now in the developing countries. Don't need it. Throw it out the window.

But back in 1969, as with many other western countries, the government took leadership. Suddenly the penny dropped. Our eyes were opened to what we were doing. We changed. Our highways for one, have since been transformed for the better.

As individuals we can all make an effort to do the right thing to care for our environment. As individual nations we can do the right thing. But without global leadership, our individual effort is not doing much more than giving us a warm and fuzzy feeling.

And that's the key point here. We've become consumed with this emotional debate on climate change. Conveniently used by politicians for point scoring arguments of one side against the other. But who cares? It doesn't take a rocket scientist or an expert climate change scientist to see what we are doing. Plastic waste along with all the other forms of water, land and air pollution, is getting out of control. Our personal backyards may be well kept, but the reality is we all know that what we consume means our global waste is growing exponentially. Our out of sight, out of mind attitude is quickly catching up with us.

Instead, we need to shift our energy, not on a climate change

CHAPTER 21: CLIMATE CHANGE, WHO CARES?

debate as to who's right and who's wrong, but on to addressing the core of the problem, the pollution we generate. If nothing more, we could aim to leave our planet as we found it, not a worse mess for our future generations. While the problem seems insurmountable, it's easy to ignore. But we can affect change. Like all social change, sharing the conversation will lead to making a difference. In the meantime, we may still continue polluting our global backyard and tossing our waste away with abandoned disregard. But hopefully, it won't be too long before our political leaders, those with global influence, including those who currently don't give a toss, may be influenced by a growing collective conversation. To start providing the required global leadership.

Nature not only gives us an incredible and diverse spectacle to admire but like that landlord, continues to provide us with generous and forgiving abundance. Would we feel comfortable about our future generations remembering us as one of the tenants from hell?

We live in an amazing world. We can make a difference. Watch the video. Start the conversation. If you think this message helps, share the story. Share the video.

So, if for no other reason, by the time yours or my young grandkids travel around the world in their latter midlife, hopefully they too will still be able to enjoy the extraordinary experience nature offers. If not, just that bit cleaner.

There's no waste in Singapore. What a model city.

Chapter 22

A DARK PAST. BUT THERE'S STILL MUCH TO SMILE ABOUT

Yesterday are memories. Tomorrow is a mystery. Today is a gift. Taken from a saying discovered in a Cambodian market. A great youthful midlife travel principle. Completely unplanned. Freewheeling from day to day. Or at best week to week. Picking up advice from other travellers and planning as you go. Such is the reason I ventured to Cambodia. The first country in South East Asia of the final stage of my around the world adventure.

Phnom Penh is an appealing place to visit. There are extensive cultural and historical attractions. No shortage of temples or museums. Plus, there's an excellent range of dining venues. The Mekong River provides an attractive backdrop to the city as with many of the expansive, well presented and maintained parks.

After backpacking for six months, I thought it's time to revert back to Plan A. Use Phnom Penh as a base. This seemed like a nice city. Stay in one place for the last few months of the trip. That idea lasted five days. Maybe it was the certain culture of the downtown area I was staying in. Sure, the city offers a vibrant and varied nightlife. But as one young backpacker remarked, this place is full of old, grey haired men with young Cambodian girls. Then add very cheap beer into the mix. It's unquestionably a very popular destination for a segment of the tourism market. But for me, I was now happy to revert to Plan B. Backpacking my way further into Asia still had a lot of appeal. Admittedly, further out from the downtown part of the city, there is a different picture. Appealing leafy residential apartment areas that cater for the more longer term expat community. But my stay wasn't quite that long.

No matter what part of the city, one thing stood out. You can see why Cambodians have a reputation for smiling. Have you ever noticed people sitting alone in a café? Their faces long and expressionless. All of a sudden, from out of nowhere, their face will light up. A smirk appears. It grows, from ear to ear. Aaah, you discover. They're tapping away on their phone. The cycle of smirking continues with each bling bling sound bringing the next message. Sort of like remote control smiling. Fascinating to watch!

In Cambodia, I made up my own version of a smiley face game. It's a simple game. I use the back of a tuk tuk. I've played it riding around the streets of Phnom Penh. Just look for someone while the tuk tuk is waiting at the lights. They'll have their similar, just going about their daily business expression on their face. All you do is just throw a genuine warm smile at them. And then, watch it come back. There was this one older guy. His smile was so infectious, every wrinkle on his warm but age-weathered face seemed to open up into a broad smile. It is said the Cambodian smile is an inner smile that represents harmony and spirituality. Whatever the reason, it's heart-warming.

CHAPTER 22: A Dark Past. But There's Still Much to Smile About

Cambodia has a rich history. But unfortunately, this has been overshadowed by a more recent dark and gruesome period of the Pol Pot Khmer Rouge regime. Not even the Cambodians believe this could have happened to them. A period of just over three years where almost a quarter of their population lost their lives. Lost either directly by execution, or indirectly by torture or starvation. And we are only talking about a period as recent as 1975 to 1979.

Interestingly, there seem to be parallels to the history pages of other regions as with a number of Latin American countries. Profiteering by foreign national interest, propped up dictators to protect those foreign economic and political interests. Large pockets of the community being degraded to extreme poverty. With nothing to lose, joining what develops as extremist groups. The rest is history. Unfortunately, Pol Pot's ideals of creating the perfect communal society got destructively out of hand.

And that's one of the main reasons Cambodians support these sombre, and I must say, near stomach churning museum sites. An attempt to never forget. To not let this ever happen again.

There was one relatively lighter side of a story featured at the Genocide Museum in Phnom Penh. It's about a New Zealand yachty, Kerry Hamill. Before his execution he wanted to make sure he would have the last say. In his confession he stated that Colonel Sanders, of Kentucky Fried Chicken fame, was one of his superiors. He used his family home telephone number as his CIA operative number. He mentioned several family friends as supposed members of the CIA. For instance, Colonel Perram was his father's gliding instructor. He also mentions a Captain Pepper which no doubt was reference to the Beetle's album. He mentioned a Major Rouse. A ruse in English is a fraud or a confidence trick. Perhaps the most poignant comment in his confession was the mention of a public speaking instructor, a Mr S. Tarr. This was in fact the name of his adoring mother, Esther Hamill. He was no doubt sending a final message to his mother.

Sadly, with the likes of the Hitlers and other such misaligned forms of human influencers that sporadically surface throughout human history, we can only hope the impact could never be anywhere as horrible as this chapter.

Despite such a devastating chapter of their past, you can't help but have so much more respect for the Cambodian people. Their resilience and determination, particularly the young generation, to move forward.

Because that's the sense you feel as you make your way around the likes of Phnom Penh. Matching those smiley faced people, is a bright, clean and tidy vibrant city. Sure, there's the Sydney Kings Crossy nightlife side of the city with its extensive choice of bars and associated entertainment that goes with it. But beyond this you find vibrant, modern and sophisticated residential communities with a growing number of high-end developments.

It just goes to prove, that no matter what horrific adversity may shadow your past, there's still lots to smile about. Cambodians are proof of that. Like Cambodia has experienced, life is full of extremes. From extreme suffering to boundless joy and hope.

As was the experience in northern Thailand. It reminded me of an Australian drought. The relentless scorching heat year after year, where every conceivable amount of life is sucked out of the parched land. There seems no hope. The only thing the lifelessness of the earth grows is deep furrows of despair.

But then something amazing happens. Out of nowhere the

CHAPTER 22: A Dark Past. But There's Still Much to Smile About

rains come. And what was lifeless and useless land, suddenly flourishes to the most amazing bountiful landscape of plants and flowers. It's like a miracle. Such is the life of the Australian outback.

It was far from a drought in northern Thailand. But the feeling of despair and hopelessness was once the same. There was no parched land. But for the Hilltribe people there was the same spirit of hope that lay deep within. Just like that forgotten land. Waiting to flourish. The unseen power within. The power that transforms life.

I spent a week with the Hilltribe people in the mountains north of the country. A population of about four hundred thousand. Many have no national ID and therefore cannot travel. Most are extremely poor. Combined with a lack of education, the girls are commonly traded by human traffickers. Typically, the "Karaoke" Bars. The beginning of the end. Next stop Bangkok. You know those nightclubs we've joked about how those girls entertain the crowd. That could have been one of our daughters. Take a peep through the door of one of those notorious bars. It's more saddening than enticing. In particular, after learning where many of these young girls come from, I'd rather be entertained by two flies crawling up a wall than the glitzy masquerade of this industry's dark side.

So prevalent is the human trafficking, some villages have no girls left. Then there's the drug trade. The need to get amphetamines across the border down through Bangkok. The Hilltribe people once again become the target.

But there is hope. Organisations like the Borderless Friendship Foundation. Their efforts may be just making a small dent. But it's a tremendous start. Giving these Hilltribe children hope. A future. Over sixty percent of the children on the five hostels supported by the foundation are effectively orphans. Either without parents,

parents lost to drugs or abandoned by their parents.

Like that forgotten dry parched desert. You can't see the human spirit. You can't touch it. But nurture it and watch it blossom. Like Bovi, this young boy of three. You could almost see the pain of his past through his young eyes. But what you felt more was this delightful joy-inspiring personality blossoming with each day as a result of the caring people now nurturing him. The kind of love and affection most of us take for granted.

And the results are continuing to show. That's apart from the joy and sense of hope and opportunity you see on these kids' faces. It's also showing in their school results. Once discarded by the broader community as without hope, some of these Hilltribe children are now outranking the local kids.

It's through individual sponsorship, generous contributions by businesses and organisations like Rotary International who are supporting their life changing opportunity.

How the decision of two mining companies in Australia are changing the lives of Hilltribe children in northern Thailand.

And that's what brought me here. The story from the early part of my journey. Where in a remote part of Australia, I learnt, because of a downturn, large mining companies were dumping good used bed linen. Thanks to the Rotary Club of Mill Point in Perth, they identified a number of charities who would benefit. The end result being about fifty thousand items of quality bed linen, worth a replacement value of around a half million Australian dollars (approx. US$350,000), distributed to people in need.

CHAPTER 22: A Dark Past. But There's Still Much to Smile About

One of those benefiting charities was the Borderless Friendship Foundation here in northern Thailand. We may take for granted the linen we sleep on. But for these kids their gratitude is heart-warming. So, like the magic that lies within the harsh Australian land, maybe that linen from the outback may help bring out just a bit more of that magic human spirit that lies within each of those children. The Borderless Friendship Foundation is certainly giving them every chance, in so many ways.

The extremes of human nature. From the gruesome to the delightful.

Chapter 23

THE CONFESSIONS OF A MIDLIFE BACKPACKER

What's interesting are the parallels South East Asia has to Spain and Latin America. In Latin America, every town proudly parades their town square and Iglesia (Catholic church) as the main tourist feature. Here it's the temples. But no matter the religious or cultural differences, whether Catholic, Jewish, Buddhist or Hindu, there's one common trend. That is how younger generations are edging away from fully adhering to long held traditional customs. The change in pre-marriage relationships is a widespread example, as one young Buddhist explained to me the conflict with his family.

Even so, as with all cultures, religious influence runs deep and has very much shaped our customs, traditions and beliefs. For example, Buddhism may typically be seen as being all about peace and mindfulness. But generosity through giving is also a very key part of Buddhism. As a Buddhist explained, one of the biggest benefits of giving in Buddhism is Karma. As with taking care of your parents, he went on to explain. When they pass on, they will provide you protection. If for example, he said, you are lost in the forest and become fearful, you know they will protect you. That means you no longer have to deal with the crippling results of fear but can then better deal with the situation. I like that one. It's all about the mindset.

It's unquestionable though, the influence religion has on our cultures. How it has shaped our history through to our current time. Siem Reap in Cambodia is one example. "Grander than anything left to us by Greece or Rome" is how one historian described Angkor Wat. The biggest temple in the world. Confession one. I never knew that. But impressive it is. The grandeur and sheer scale of it.

They certainly didn't sit around idly back then in the 12th century I reasoned, as I wandered and climbed around the site, along with thousands of Chinese tourists. You can't help but marvel at the construction and the huge amount of resources that would have been required to construct it. And the more recent attempts to keep parts of it propped up. But there's something I clearly missed. As Collete, an English lady I was talking with, later explained to me. She not only saw what I saw, but she felt it as well. The spiritual energy. So much so she was moved to tears at times.

Next confession coming up….

One of the most liberating aspects of a more youthful style of midlife travel is the flexibility. Not having to drag along the ball and chain. No, I'm not talking about the missus! That I do miss. No, a suitcase. Just a backpack. Only two of everything. No more. Yet small enough to get away as carry-on luggage. The only compromise is the extended days of wear…until it fails the sniff test.

CHAPTER 23: The Confessions of a Midlife Backpacker

Most nights I do a laundry foot stomp wash in the shower, followed by a rinse in the sink. Hang it out to dry overnight and if it passes the sniff test, it's good to go. The problem is, I'm getting conscious of being seen to have brought just one set of clothes… like why does he even need a backpack? The thing is, unless you walk past mirrors all day, you don't actually get to see more than mere glimpses of your outfit. And travelling solo, you don't have anyone telling you, "you're not wearing that again are you?"

The problem is the photos tell another story. It starts to appear that in fact, you really did only take one set of clothes. But if the photos are a concern, a simple photo shop edit makes it easy to at least change the colour of your shirt for example. "Oh wow," you would have people saying, "You must have taken a huge wardrobe with you."

Photoshopping aside, my criteria is good quality, light weight, quick dry clothes. Easy to wash out each night. No more than two of each: socks, undies, shirt, shorts. Zip off legs for one of the shorts. Good quality walking shoes. And a lightweight jumper. This seems a bit odd in the tropics. But it's definitely a life saver in mountainous regions or when the temperature is set low in buses, planes and trains.

After all this, the backpack weighs in close to 10kg, 3k over the carry-on luggage limit. Bummer. Really, this whole weight limit is a joke. Now I'd shed close to 10kg prior to the trip, but does that count? Oh no. So, let's say I'm checking in alongside this really huge 200kg guy with carry-on luggage of just 1kg. Here comes me at a fraction of my friend's weight, but my bag, 3kg over the carry-on limit. "Oh, through you go Mr Huge Albert, while I attend to Mr Bean Pole with his irresponsible carry-on luggage weight." But don't worry, I was ready for their little game.

I don't know about you, but sometimes I can get these really cold flushes. Like if I had one of these attacks when checking in, there would be only one solution. Put on every piece of clothing I could take out of my bag. Of course, flight staff I'm sure would be quite cynical about my personal dilemma. Maybe because I not only would look like the Michelin tyre man but be starting to sweat like a pig. Reminds me of that airline scene in the movie, "Something about Mary," I could just see them on the plane. There they'd be standing next to me in the aisle with an excess luggage credit card machine in one hand and the aircraft temperature control in the other hand, as they slowly wound the temperature up to try and break me.

It's all about the timing though. That's why I always timed my laundry after a flight. Let's imagine I have a bag full of clothes that hadn't passed the sniff test. I would dare say they would be saying, stuff your cold sweats and be pleading with me to take them all off again and put them back in the bag. So I reckon I had this carry-on luggage issue sorted.

But when you've got a bag full of clothes that no matter how much foot stomping, the sniff test fails, it's time to seek external help. Which brings me to my next confession.

Things are fantastically cheap here. A lovely resort style room for just over twenty bucks. A cocktail at a dollar fifty. Same for a packet of cigarettes, if that's your thing. And best of all, a beer for as low as fifty cents. And when the sniff test fails, fortunately there's the laundry service, washed dried and folded for just a dollar a kilo. It just so happened the local laundry doubles as a hairdresser. For two dollars a cut. Smart operator this laundry

CHAPTER 23: The Confessions of a Midlife Backpacker

lady. Only intended to drop in the washing. Next I knew I was all draped up having a haircut.

I find getting a haircut is a way to really experience the local culture. You never know what you'll end up with. The challenge I find is when gesturing with a small gap between your fingers saying "little, little", you never know whether they understand that to mean what is intended to just cut a little, or to only leave a little.

My hairdresser was a charming, smallish lady. This may have been a laundry, but it was clear she loved her craft. Being of small stature, I could see she was struggling to reach the top of my head. I figured either the chair was at its lowest or it was broken. So, I slumped as far down in the chair I could manage, much to her immediate expression of delight.

After several passes over my head I was starting to accept that what she understood was to leave little. At least, I consoled myself, I was still capable of growing hair. She gestured the eye brows. I have learnt to appreciate over the years that women have a dislike for any wayward male hair follicles. I could sense my hair dresser was clearly no different. Before I knew it, she had moved on from the eye brows and now had half her clippers jammed in my left ear canal. She was on a mission. As she prodded and poked her buzzing clippers in and out of my ear, I was convinced she must have discovered one stubborn follicle that she was determined to master.

I could understand where she was coming from. I know what it's like when you have an obsessive determination. Like trying to jag that last remaining tiny spring onion from the bottom of a jar. I'm just so thankful she didn't start on my nostrils. I'd still be there.

This experience wasn't about to end here, though. What she offered next just made sense. If the clothes were to finally get a decent wash, then I reasoned a bit extra for a hair wash and scrub made good sense.

I call this the Bali syndrome. Everything is so cheap. Until you go home with everything, you realise it wasn't such a cheap trip after all. Which is what I later figured was the trap I had now found myself in. So, we've now got clean clothes, a haircut, plus gleaming hair. Obviously, there's just one thing missing. A face massage. Clearly neither here nor there I thought. But it's only when well into this latest offering, the focus shifted. That's when the face mask was applied. Ok so yes, I'm going to have to admit. I will confess, I had a facial!

One last confession… Say you were travelling on a bus enroute to cross through the border into another country. There's the cost of the visa entry. You suddenly realise you lost your wallet. Ok so yes, I confess, I lost my wallet. Hit me like a brick it did. Not the wallet. I would have been quite happy if that happened. But just the thought. The implications of what I now found myself in. Couldn't believe it. I'm constantly doing the three way tap check. Wallet, passport, phone. Check. I'm convinced I was pick-pocketed. Not so hard on the confession too, that way.

But let's say you either had to lose your passport, phone or wallet. Which would you choose? Well thankfully for me, it was my wallet. Now don't get me wrong, suddenly being penniless with no credit card, stuck on a bus in the middle of unfamiliar Asian countryside with a bus full of non-English speaking locals is a daunting feeling. The thought of being left stranded at the border, my outlook suddenly shifted from a cruisy day to dealing with this

CHAPTER 23: The Confessions of a Midlife Backpacker

new challenge. Apart from being in the middle of nowhere, it was a Saturday. As such no chance of finding any financial institution such as a bank open. Fortunately, I did discover a sympathetic young Swedish traveller who was willing to exchange a hundred dollar bill for an international bank transfer I did via my phone.

This did at least allow me to get through the border and get by for a day. I was now waiting, waiting for MasterCard's "Emergency" cash. As the days slipped by, the prospect of living under a tree in a foreign country eating nuts, berries and leaves was an unnerving one. But what happened next was like one of those rags to riches stories. This time I was living it.

Laos was never on my destination list. You think of South East Asia and either Vietnam or Thailand immediately rises to the top. Most people don't even know where Laos is.

Unfortunately, it's another one of those countries with a dark past. Laos has been the most heavily bombed country per capita in history. For nine years to 1973, the U.S.A. dropped the equivalent to a planeload of bombs every 8 minutes, 24 hours a day on the country.

I'd heard along the way about this city in the north of the country. I couldn't even pronounce the name. But the inside information was you have to go there. And that's what I did. And what I found was probably one of the nicest places I'd visited on this trip. Luang Prabang.

Luang Prabang has a magical blend of French influence infused into Asia. Now I don't care what the English say about the French. But you gotta give it to the French. They got taste. And that's what they left behind here back in the 19th century. Luang Prabang is outstanding for both its rich architectural and artistic heritage. You soon experience this just walking around the streets. With the Mekong River winding its way around the city, it's at night when its beauty really shines. The streets lined with restaurants and guest houses come to life at nightfall as the trees and buildings tastefully light up. Blending together with the tropical night air to form the perfect setting to dine or chat over a drink. The city thankfully doesn't have the pub street partying atmosphere of the more popular tourist hot spots. Instead a slower paced ambience that not only glistens at night but entices a casual meandering stroll or bicycle ride through its streets. Stopping off for a coffee at a French patisserie or a beer in a bar, if not just simply to take it all in.

It's clearly been a well-kept secret. Fellow Perth Rotarian club members have been coming to Laos for years through their Global Hands Charity organisation. They've shown me photos of them mixing cement, building dormitories, handing out hearing aids to deaf kids, fixing bicycles. Totally dedicated and admirable voluntary work they do. But showing me photos of Luang Prabang, as I only now found out they've been going to. Oh no. Not a word about Luang Prabang. Clearly there's been a pact to keep this secret well under wraps. Maybe it's because they too discovered the millionaire lifestyle I suddenly found myself in.

It may have taken a while but when MasterCard finally delivered, I too was suddenly liv'n the life. From penniless to the life of a multimillionaire. At one point I peaked at 2.6 million. Suddenly I found out what it was like living the life of the high rollers. If a top quality coffee cost a few grand, so what. Dining in one of the most beautiful settings you could imagine on the water's edge. Another ten grand here and there. It was there to be enjoyed.

CHAPTER 23: The Confessions of a Midlife Backpacker

I was now also obviously amongst the elite and famous in this well-kept secret Asian hideaway. Like world famous Kama Sutra. I realised that early one morning when I discovered he was staying in the room above me. I was woken suddenly just before 4am. Like most of the guest houses, they are a wooden construction. He was either just getting home or, was just firing up. Now there are no chandeliers in our rooms. But clearly that wasn't stopping our friend Kama Sutra. I soon learned there were more creative uses of floor boards than I could have ever imagined. Each move of his manly prowess boomed from the building like a giant boom box blasting across the town into the still air of the night.

But just like ol' Kama Sutra in the room above me, all good things eventually come to an end. It was also time for me to leave. And so was my millionaire lifestyle. I still had a million left. But after exchanging back to dollars, I wondered where else my now hundred dollars may once again bulge my pocket with such sudden wealth. If not at least to once again provide that same millionaire feeling.

One of the attractions about South East Asia is the low cost of travelling. At least thirty percent cheaper than Latin America. Buses have proven again a great way to travel within countries and between countries. But one form of transport that Central America and South America don't have are trains.

I like trains. One of my more memorable train trips was fifteen years ago. I'm not sure why, but for some reason I decided I would sing to my wife on our 25th anniversary. As it turned out, this would be while crossing Australia's Nullarbor desert on the Indian Pacific train. Not just a verse, but the full gig. And two songs at that. Even our zany neighbour next door got into the act as well. Not for the final show, but the lessons.

Unfortunately, after two singing courses, the only result I got from all this was how much I now appreciate the talent of a good singer. And how much practice it takes to make a really good singer. I did fulfill my promise though. She was so gracious!! There was however, some further use made of all this talent training. Together with the neighbour and mate Tone, we performed at private functions. Very private. Only very late at night. And only when ours and our audience's senses were sufficiently numbed.

Taking a train is like flying used to be. Turn up at the gate five minutes before departure. No security hassles. No having to unpack your bag to discard that stray oversized shampoo bottle or drag your laptop out. Get undressed. Take your shoes off. Belt. Empty your pockets. Be intimidated with arms outstretched while you're x-rayed. Then get dressed again, stuffing your travel essentials back in your pockets.

But there's one security test I will confess I go out of my way to avoid. It's become a little game for me. It all started when a new airport opened in Adelaide, South Australia. The new staff were obviously trained specifically on what to say and how to respond. It was that bomb test. That routine where they swipe over your bag and then stick the swipe in a machine. They always ask, "Are you willing to do the test"? So, I says, "Yep". She repeats the question, "Are you willing to do the test"? I reply the same, "Yep". She asks again. Same reply. This time, clearly becoming a little irritated, she asks, "Can't you say yes". I say "Nope", now trying to think what to say next, so I advise, "It's a speech impediment". She advises she will need to get her supervisor if I can't say "yes".

CHAPTER 23: The Confessions of a Midlife Backpacker

I agree. A couple of minutes later, she returns with the supervisor. She informs the supervisor, "He's got a speech impediment and can't say yes," as I'm struggling to ensure I keep a straight face. They go to the side to discuss this predicament. Clearly, this was not covered in their training manual. They return to advise, yes, they would accept this response. True story. I notice "Yep" has since been an accepted form of response.

Hence why I now play the game of looking over the shoulder to time the escape past this one final security hassle.

The beauty is in places like Chiang Mai, you can avoid all that inconvenience and frustration. Take a relaxing modern and comfortable overnight sleeper berth train at the end of your day. First thing next morning be in Bangkok, ready to go.

It was only going to be a couple of days in northern Thailand. But that extended closer to a couple of weeks. Getting involved with the local community is always the cream on the travel cake. It was satisfying to have the opportunity to contribute as well. Setting up some online marketing for their enterprising Hilltribe tourism venture. If you're visiting Thailand be sure to include chiangdaobasecamp.com on your itinerary.

Bangkok by comparison is quite the contrast. It's easy to dismiss it, as some describe, a sleaze city. But step away from those sordid parts of the city, and let's be honest, every city has them, and you find Bangkok offers an endless cultural feast to whet any visitor's appetite. Whether that's taking one of the very popular leisurely half day cycle tours around the city. Stopping here and there for a drink. Getting an insight into the local history from your guide. Or enjoying an all time favourite dish of Pad Thai. Not forgetting one of the signature dishes that defines Thai flavour, a bowl of spicy favourite Yum Tom. Yuuum yum. Then there's the colour and vibrancy you'll discover in one of the many night markets. And of course, the infamous must-see weekend market that sells everything from pots and pans to the treats from the icecream maker entertaining the crowd as he bangs and claps to the music churning out another tasty delight.

And no visit would be complete without a tour of one or two or three or four, or…more, of the many elaborate and ornate temples. If you find yourself wondering why just about every visitor wears those baggy daggy elephant pants around town, I just discovered a good reason. You need long pants to tour the King's Palace. For a few bucks they pack well in the backpack anyway.

For me, well I'm culturally topped up thank you. Must go. Have that train to catch…

From Cambodia to Laos, to Thailand.
There's so much to see.

Chapter 24

THE FAMILY VACATION. YOU CAN'T BEAT 'EM

I've always had this theory. No matter how grandiose or want for nothing a palatial home you've got, you still need to get away. And we'll typically go to great lengths to achieve that.

As a child of the fifties and sixties it was the family caravan. That half-moon shaped dome on wheels. Towed behind the family car to the favourite beach side resort. Ah, yes. The great Aussie getaway. There we'd be parked in the blistering summer heat. The whole family squeezed into our little mobile baking box. All these little boxes lined up one after another packed into the foreshore caravan park. Sunburnt by day. Sweltering by night.

Fast forward fifty, sixty years. The concept hasn't changed. But things have gotten a little more comfortable. The family car is now more an air-conditioned lounge on wheels. "Riddle me riddle me ree there's something I can see," has been replaced with each child's own personal video entertainment system. Marital conflicts over map reading directions have been resolved with an onboard navigation system.

But there's one big, additional difference now. Choice.

The world has since become a lot smaller. It's now just as cheap for the whole family to grab a flight to some exotic overseas location.

The great thing about family holidays is they create memories. Memories that last a lifetime. And it's not memories from when everything goes perfectly. It's all the little unexpected things that go wrong.

Like the family decides to take a tuk tuk ride. The first thing you need to adapt to, standards are different to home. A tuk tuk ride is a bit like a roller coaster ride but without the rails. You never know what's going to happen next. Like half way into the journey along the main road. The whole family, along with grandpa are all packed into this little three wheeled open air sidecar type machine. The motor starts to splutter. Tuk Tuk and all its passengers come to a sudden halt. Fortunately, as it turns out, it's not that far to push Tuk Tuk and all its passengers to a nearby gas station.

One of the attractive things about such an exotic getaway are the cheap massages. A whole hour's massage for a mere fraction you'd pay back home. The family that massages together stays together. This must have been the thinking at the time. Or perhaps the bulk rate that slashed the price even lower.

So, here we all are. Baby in pusher, in theory, asleep for the whole duration. And thank goodness for ten fingers and ten toe nails. There's a good hour's worth of nail painting entertainment for the other little family member. Meanwhile mum, dad and grandpa have all settled in. All lined up on our masseur tables. Curtains drawn enough to suggest some discreetness but

CHAPTER 24: The Family Vacation. You Can't Beat 'Em

looking more like a hospital emergency department.

I'm not sure what the selection process was. But the masseur I was allocated was the considerably more mature aged of all the women. Actually, she reminded me of an Asian version of my grandmother. While trying to avoid any prolonged eye contact, I pondered if she had perhaps taken up this job as a twilight career change, or was used as like a last minute emergency department fill in. I figured the latter was more probable.

I have to say, granny was good at her craft. It was probably only fifteen minutes into this relaxing slumber like state. I say slumber, because the last thing I remember was my foot being soothingly massaged. But suddenly I woke with a jolt. In horror, I find granny now perched on my back. Strutting up and down it as if I'm a paddle board. This is where the happy family experience took a sudden turn. I'm not sure if it was my sudden awakening jolt, but next thing baby wakes up with an almighty scream. So, there's me coming to terms with granny knee boarding on my back, baby screaming. Meanwhile instructions are coming out left right and centre from the adjoining cubicles in a desperate attempt to console baby. A unique massage experience with a difference. But it's "moments like these" that makes family time very special. But for grandpa, I feel extra special just to be a part of it.

Thailand has been a special part of this journey. Enjoying the tropical beach areas south of the country with some of my family members has been extra special. I was seeking a visionary look into the future. So, before we all departed, I asked my young granddaughter what she would like to be when she's old, like Poppa. Not sure I should take it as a compliment or not, but a super hero was her response.

It's always an interesting question what the next fifty years would be like. On social attitudes, one of my favourite questions, is the what were we thinking question. In fifty years, what will be the what were we thinking issue we think is now normal?

Looking back, one of the most embarrassing of them all, Australia's then White Australia Policy. Attitudes to mental health. I was having a beer with a backpacker as he talked about how mental health issues like the depression he was managing, can now be more openly discussed. Gay relationships. At least we have progressed as a society to be more open and accepting. And while a large part of the world has already moved on, I wonder whether Australia's requirement to vote on gay marriage will be another one of those what were we thinking issues.

And then there's the impact of technology. It's mind boggling to think that in the space of around a mere ten years our communication with each other has so drastically changed. No matter what corner of the globe, no matter how poor, there's a smart phone in hand. Expect Maslow's Hierarchy of Basic Needs to be soon updated to be air, food, drink, smartphone, shelter, etc.

I was discussing the impact of social media with the manager of a Thailand island resort. In days past all his bookings came through travel agencies. Now it's social media booking sites. He said the impact is dramatic. Bad reviews will impact his bookings within days. And vice versa. But that's only been the last five years. What will sixty years' time bring? In this small Thai coffee shop, I was blown away when my mugshot, via an app was instantly printed on my coffee. I expect in the future, an app won't even be required.

CHAPTER 24: The Family Vacation. You Can't Beat 'Em

We're being warned artificial Intelligence is set to displace many current jobs. I speculated this issue with a young Thai founder of a new tourism venture. Losing that Thai service with a smile just wouldn't be the same though.

The world has unquestionably become so much smaller. The ease and convenience of communicating with the likes of that smartphone is only helping to further shrink the globe. The extent of travel by young backpackers, their confidence, is to be applauded and encouraged…along with the need for more midlife backpackers! Outback Jack back in Costa Rica, summed it up well. The more we travel and connect with people of other nations, in particular for young people, the more we will understand that no matter where we are from, we are all much the same. In doing so we can also discover that what we are often led to believe, may in fact not necessarily be in all our best interests after all. Wars are a typical example.

Meanwhile as a case in point, we muse at a couple of our global clowns spruiking at each other as to who's got the biggest nuke. Instead of banging the war drums, could it be possible to unite together to fight our common threat. One that we have all created. So we can all leave our global home in just a bit better state for our next generations.

But then again, instead of the antics of our current global leaders, maybe we really do need super heroes to pull it off. Even if it does mean it will be another one of those what were we thinking issues.

Thank you, Thailand, for the special family times.

 Thailand. A delightful tropical escape.

Chapter 25

IN SEARCH OF HORSE CART 101

We thought it was a hell of a joke. I grew up in a small country highway siding town in southern Australia. It was known then as the Ninety Mile Desert. The problem was there wasn't a lot to do at night. But my brother and I figured it would be the highlight of our week if we nicked one of those solid wooden, white posts from the side of the highway. Better still we'd sneak it into our parents' bedroom while they slept. Oh what a surprise it'd be when they woke up!

I was reminded of that little story when here in Myanmar, or Burma as it was known. The story here goes back to the 1820s. In this case, British soldiers were busy plundering the Shwedagon Pagoda. They too, no doubt thought it would be a huge joke to nick this 23 ton bronze bell from the local pagoda. Problem was, enroute to Calcutta, the bell fell overboard and sank into the sea. At least we returned our prized haul the next day. The Brits left it to the locals to later recover their bell. It now sits atop the pagoda platform.

Now there's pagodas and there's pagodas. But even for those overdosed on pagodas, the Shwedagon Pagoda in Yangon, home of the infamous bell, is impressive. It's like a village of gold featuring an endless collection of Buddhas of all sizes. The pagoda however, represents just a small proportion of the country's Buddhas. With a Myanmar population of 53 million, it is suggested the number of Buddhas is ten times that.

Yangon has been described by some as a smaller Bangkok. It certainly has the similar big Asian city traits. The sprawling market centres, streets lined with food stalls and merchandise along with those distinctive Asian street smells.

Further north, Bagan offers a totally different feel. It's dusty streets...well, before it got drenched with flooding rains, give it an almost rural feel. Yet it's big enough to offer the full range of good quality services such as accommodation and restaurants. It has a certain casual, easy going attraction about the place you feel as soon as you arrive.

Bagan was once the capital of the prosperous Bagan empire, around the 11th and 13th century. The empire featured a massive 10,000 temples and pagodas. Today, about 2,200 structures remain. It is famous for being one of the most dense concentrations of temples and pagodas in the world. It certainly looks it, too. There are temples and pagodas all over the place, in all shapes and sizes.

It's not just the huge number of temples scattered across the landscape that stand out. It's also the even greater number of ebikes that have taken over the region. If video killed the radio star, the ebike has almost annihilated the once popular traditional horse and cart. Apparently only within the last three years. Truckloads

CHAPTER 25: In Search of Horse Cart 101

of ebikes from China came down. Now almost every street corner rents ebikes. By contrast, the occasional horse and cart plods slowly along, dodging ebikes zipping in all directions past them.

The horse and cart however, offered an interesting twist to my stay here. Seventeen years ago my daughter, then working for a travel agent, visited Burma. She was asked to deliver a gift to Horse Cart 101. It was a watch and an English Dictionary from a customer. Apparently, Ko Ko the owner, burst into tears when he received it. I was curious.

I made it a mission to find Horse Cart 101. I eventually tracked down Horse Cart 101. And he still remembered the gift. A video link back to Nicole was a nice warm touch to finish the search. They agreed both were a bit older, but Ko Ko now spoke near perfect English. To complete the story, the search is now on for the customer who provided the gift.

Meanwhile, business is certainly a lot quieter for Horse Cart 101. But I wait with much interest to see if in fact Horse Cart 101's fortunes could be turned around? I sort of felt for Ko Ko and the dilemma of all his fellow horse carts. It's a bit like that classic business case study from the eighteen hundreds. What business are we in? When rail came along and horse carriages were put out of business as they were replaced with rail carriages. If you can't beat 'em, join 'em. I questioned Ko Ko with various alternative concepts. Sometimes new ideas are a bit like "borrowing" a white post, or a bell…they just need to be taken from somewhere else. We'll wait and see.

There's a certain mystique about Myanmar. Its rich history that goes back 13,000 years. Its rich treasures of temples, pagodas and stupas spread across the landscape. A mix of gleaming gold domed structures that jut through the trees. The ancient remains that turn rich red with each setting of the sun.

A country that like so many, but perhaps more so, has endured a long history of conflict and internal ethnic disputes. Yet its people radiate a certain enduring, patient and charming quality.

A relaxing twelve hour boat journey up the huge Irrawaddy River from Bagan brings you to the bustling city of Mandalay. In many areas along the river, recent flooding reveals just the roof tops of thatched homes. A farmer guides his cattle across the extremely wide river. The farmer is in his boat. The cattle alongside the boat swim frantically from one side of the bank to the other.

You can't help but admire the resourcefulness of people in these countries. Whether it's that farmer transporting his cattle to market, a satellite dish strapped to a chair or three stories high of goods stacked on a motor bike. That's what you gotta love about these places…no shortage of innovation. It's like we were a couple of generations back where we also had to overcome problems with much more basic resources. Like my grandfather who cut a hole in his shearing shed floor so he could still crutch (shear) sheep because one of his legs was amputated.

Or my uncle's farm ute (pickup truck) that kept boiling because the radiator was blocked. No problem. He bypassed the plumbing from the radiator to a forty-four gallon drum of water he placed on the back of the ute. Even his drum got to boiling point, but he got by. That must have inspired me. It was just after we were married. We were towing a twenty two foot caravan. The temperature was well into the forties centigrade. It was too much

CHAPTER 25: In Search of Horse Cart 101

for the car as it kept overheating. Solution: A hose connected to the caravan's water pump was used to spray water down the radiator. Worked a treat while it got us home.

But here in Mandalay the second largest city in Burma, life is still even simpler. Resources more basic. Step outside of the city and you are taken back further in time. Oxen still plough the fields. Water is carted from the village well. Horse carts bump and clip clop their way along the uneven rough tracks.

Mandalay is a former royal capital. Home to the Mandalay Palace, surrounded by a moat, it now serves as one of the city's main tourist attractions. The city is known for its cultural diversity. Half of Burma's monks live in Mandalay and surrounding areas.

Several hours further north is the laid-back town of Hsipaw, located high in the hills of the Shan State. Its usually dusty streets and traditional buildings present a more laid back and relaxed atmosphere. It's from here our five-hour trek begins. Through the mountains of north eastern Myanmar. Our destination for the night, a remote village, five hours away.

The path works its way through the villages of the Shan people, vegetable crops, paddies, natural streams and springs. Continuing up the mountain provides spectacular views across the lush green countryside. Basic timber homes and bamboo huts sparsely scatter themselves amongst the landscape mix of hillside farming, plantations, forests and rolling hills.

A stopover past a local village school provides as much excitement for the trekker. The kids come running out for a hug and a whirl. Meanwhile other kids stay focused on chanting their way through their alphabet.

After a day's trekking, no evening is complete without a story.

Sai Phyo Ko, our Burmese guide, starts to tell the story he'd been promising all day. It's a Buddhist story told from one generation of the Burmese Shan people to the next. The story tells about a villager, a farmer, a wizard and a tortoise. It's a journey where they seek Buddha's help with their problems. Like all good stories it takes a few beers and a rice wine or two to reach the end. But the moral of the story is no matter how big your problem, they are small compared to others. If we practice helping others ahead of worrying about our own, unexpectedly we magically find our problems, like karma, eventually resolved.

It must be a normal thing for tour guides. My son was a tour guide in central Australia. Around the campfire at night he would tell the story told by the Australian Aboriginals. How they believed what you do to others, such as helping them, comes back to help you. Ngapartji Ngapartji (pronounced Num-a-gee Num-a-gee) they call it.

These ancient stories reminded me of a modern version. I used to attend a number of business networking functions. The primary goal was to make as many business contacts as possible. Prospects for your business. Until one day a respected business person told a different story.

We weren't sitting in a Myanmar bamboo hut or sitting around a Central Australian outback campfire. But his message was the same. Rather than seek who can help your business, instead ask how can you help the business of someone you meet, or if you know someone who can. The universal energy doesn't forget you.

Finding the source, the authenticity of these ancient stories is difficult. Perhaps that's why they are called a secret. They are hard

CHAPTER 25: In Search of Horse Cart 101

to find. But like all good secrets to success, once you find and discover it, you find how simple the secret is. But the difficulty is not so much finding the secret, the real challenge is practicing it.

Treks in and around Myanmar are a great way to experience and get an appreciation for local village life. One of the very popular treks is from Kalaw to Inle Lake. But getting there proved interesting.

I had been waiting to meet the rest of the trekking party. The two day trek would take us through remote Myanmar villages. Suddenly a motorbike pulls up in front of me. I'm ushered to get on the back. In particular, I was instructed where to hold on. This wasn't the arrangement we had discussed with the guide the day before. Never assume, I reminded myself.

I thought we may be going a few streets away to meet the others. Instead, before I knew it we were well into the countryside. The highways here I'm sure are not much more than flattened oxen tracks with bitumen thrown over the top. The road surface challenges even the plushest of buses. For a passenger, it's like a full body massage on wheels. Or for a more vigorous work out, on the back of a motor bike, as I was experiencing.

A half hour had already passed. As we shuddered our way along our share of this highway experience at a breakneck pace, I glanced over the shoulder of the driver. I was curious of our speed. I discovered the disrepair state of the speedo was just the tip of the iceberg. It looked like half the motor bike was missing. Wires were hanging loose, some barely connected. I pondered what difference it would make if they were all connected. Part of the electrics were wrapped in a piece of dusty plastic. Even one of my foot rests was missing.

I gathered from the speed we were doing, my driver was under instruction to deliver me post haste. A destination I was yet to find out. I never got to see the face of the rider as he was wearing a full face helmet. Curious about his age, I studied his hands. I gathered by the smoothness of his skin he would have been quite young. As we overtook yet another vehicle dodging a truck coming from the opposite direction, I figured he was definitely around the invincible, I can live forever age. By contrast, it was quite clear he had no appreciation that his passenger on the back was more at the preservation age stage of life.

Helmets it seems here, are more of an optional fashion accessory. I quite like the one they wear here, the "achtung schnell schnell" German style ones, as I call them. At least my driver was wearing a helmet. That offered me some small level of comfort knowing my driver must have at least some morsel of consciousness for safety. Until I suddenly thought, "oh shit," as we continued hurtling along the highway, I was not wearing a helmet. Wasn't offered one. I could feel the grip of my hands tightening as I pondered the potential consequence. I started doing a mental check of the state of my travel insurance. If in fact, they would pay out any way. I did have a baseball cap on if that was any consolation.

I wasn't game to look down, but I was sure my knuckles were as white as. But what I couldn't help but find amazing were the locals. Casually sitting across the back seat of their bikes. As if they were sitting in a chair at home knitting. Except of course they're chatting away on their smartphone…if not also the driver. Add in a few kids perched in between mum and dad, and you've got your typical Burmese family on the move.

CHAPTER 25: In Search of Horse Cart 101

I did eventually get to meet the rest of the group. And we did arrive in one piece. I'm sure it was because of all the Buddhist temples I had visited over the last several weeks that must have released some good karma that we made it safely. Plus I was able to salvage my phone's earpiece cord that got entangled in the wheel axle! It was yet another enriching Myanmar experience. Two days trekking through the villages and mountains with a group of travellers from different nations, together experiencing more of the beauty and the culture that Myanmar offers. Experiencing an overnight stay with the monks in an ancient Buddhist monastery.

But it's the genuine friendly, warm nature of the Burmese people that captures you. They may be less governed by rules and regulations. They may be a poorer country. But they make do with what they have. To the point where a line of women cart the gravel by basket to make the roads and the cement to pave the paths. You may not always understand what's going on. But just like that trek, it all happens in the end.

Leaving this delightful country, there's one thing you can't help but take with you. It's the Burmese smile. Smile and a glowing, radiant beam of human spirit smiles back at you. Life doesn't get much simpler than that.

Sit back and enjoy of so much that Myanmar has to offer.

Chapter 26

WHAT NOW?

People often say, have you changed as a result of this journey? Let's face it, you can't change an old dog overnight, but you can certainly excite it. And there's certainly been plenty of exciting times. Living overseas as a family with our young children were major life highlights. However, the adventurous carefree nature of my trip certainly ranks up there as one of life's highlights…in a different sort of way. Different stage of life. Different circumstances.

While the question of change is best answered by observers, there's one thing I can be sure has changed. Those fears Mr Logic threw up one after another were very real. Thankfully the gut feeling stood up to it. Life is a series of stepping stones. The feeling of fear is the same. Whether it's the next unknown step that lies ahead, or that tiny step you took as a ten year old. Facing the fear to take that step ahead of you, makes the next step that much easier. So, I'm sure my journey will have made further steps into the future just that little less fearful to face.

There is one thing that has changed. That is my views on several issues. In particular, three main issues as covered in the above chapters, Drugs, Waste and Terrorism. Being exposed to others' views and experiences away from the normal and familiar surroundings, certainly brings a more heightened awareness of these issues. We all get very occupied with our lives. Travel into a completely different culture and environment disrupts that familiarity. It provides the opportunity to look outside our usual window. To question and reason more deeply about issues we would normally only give superficial thought to. Or to understand another's point of view. So yes, stepping out of the comfort zone type of travel, cannot help but change you as a person.

If I had my time again, would I do it any differently? I don't deny it would have been good to share the many experiences with someone close. But my view is, why wait? Just do it. But experiencing the same level of flexibility and freedom with a partner would be a difficult expectation. In fact, I dare say if I had done it this way with a partner, I would have ended up single anyway! Solo travelling provides a unique experience. At many times you may be alone, but personally I never felt lonely. Social media and internet connectivity make a huge difference. The ability to keep in touch almost daily with family and friends, whether a video chat or simple message, is significant.

We are social beings. We need to belong. That is nowhere more evident in many of the different cultures visited. It's why men in Myanmar are all comfortable wearing a dress. The sheet of cloth known as a Longyi. It may at first look odd to us as an outsider. But not when you are part of belonging to that group. Why women in Guatemala are identified by which village they belong to by their different coloured dress.

My tribe as I backpacked from one place to the next, in

CHAPTER 26: What Now?

between the wonderful people I met along the way, were the family and friends I was able to communicate with almost daily. And people like you whom I was able to interact with through the blog. Thank you to all of you. You made a huge difference. And of course, the so many inspiring and enjoyable people along the way. Because it's people like you who create the memories of travel.

And all this while very much being blessed with not once falling ill. Even with all the wide and varied foreign foods. And I have to say, some of the bowls of murky stuff I fronted up to... where you had no idea what was crawling below the surface. All I could say was, "come on stomach, we can do this". Not once did I ever feel in danger. With all the countries visited, including those warned not to venture into, and with all the extensive walking, not once feeling threatened or in danger.

So yes, if I had my time again, except for a few tweaks here and there I would not have changed a thing. Solo travelling was for me a first. Would I do it again? Most definitely, but probably differently. It was a unique time in life that opened up this opportunity. Life is an exciting journey. I'd be looking to make the next chapter a little different. How? Who knows? I never had plans to do a a solo backpacking trip around the world anyway.

A common concern, particularly by women, is the danger of travelling solo. You cannot deny there are dangers. But there are many female solo travellers out there. Though mainly younger. Realistically, the only sure way of avoiding danger is to not leave your house. But to me the idea of then being struck down with severe depression has less appeal. It's an individual judgement, but to me it's worth the risk. An interesting response to this question stuck in my mind. When in Costa Rica, I raised my concerns with Outback Jack about the danger of venturing further into Central America. Outback Jack, as you may recall, a past international journalist, shrugged it off. His immediate response was if they say it's dangerous there's obviously a good story there. No fear. He's obviously a few stepping stones ahead than most of us.

So, what about you? I hope sharing my journey with you, may have also inspired you. Not necessarily to do the same way I did it. Perhaps not even travel. But to do that thing you find there's been something stopping you. If you're like me, the biggest obstacle I experienced is that Mr Logic I'm here to protect you voice inside the head.

I hope your gut feeling also rises to the occasion and tells your Mr Sensible Logic to simply shut up for a change so you can go do it. Of course, it's dangerous out there. Maybe I was lucky. But I think it's far more dangerous regretting not doing it.

There's one thing that can't stop us though. It's having a youthful attitude to our midlife and beyond travel. It may be an art, but like all such skills, we get better the more we practice it.

If sharing this journey with you has inspired you in just a small way, I'm very delighted.

I'm so glad you joined me. It's been one hell of a ride. I hope you enjoyed the journey as much as I enjoyed sharing it with you. Here's to the youthful art of midlife travel....

THANKS FOR READING!

I hope this book has provided you some inspiration. Perhaps not travelling to the same extent… though I would thoroughly recommend it! But at least in some small way you may be inspired to follow your adventurous spirit.

If you gained something from the book, please share your thoughts on Facebook, Twitter or your other social media sites… or simply tell your friends! I would also welcome and very much appreciate your comments or reviews. Please go to youthfulmidlifetravel.com/review.

As a Speaker I love sharing the story. If there's an organisation or club you know who would enjoy hearing the story, please let me know (youthfulmidlifetravel.com/speaker).

If you'd like to find out more about the youthful art of midlife travel or follow the journey, please visit the web site below, check out the blog and sign up to receive updates. To learn about some of my top travel tips I used while travelling, don't forget to download my free report from the website home page.

I'd really look forward to you being part of our community where we can all be inspired to live our travel adventure dreams.

Visit:
web: www.youthfulmidlifetravel.com
email: book@youthfulmidlifetravel.com

ABOUT THE AUTHOR

Chris Herrmann was living the family dream. A family person married with three children and seven grandchildren. With a corporate management background now managing a small eCommerce business, enjoying time with family, travelling and being involved in community projects.

But life had other plans when his wife of forty years suddenly passed away as a result of cancer. The first realisation was it wasn't something that only happens to other people. The next was, while accepting his wife's journey had come to an end, his was still continuing. Coming to terms with this, he felt the need to step outside the comfort zone. To challenge himself, to see where the next stage of his life journey would take him. He decided to embark on a twelve month backpacking adventure around the world.

It was easier said than done. Facing fears of the unknown and especially leaving family and the familiar comforts of home. He wanted this trip to be about doing something completely different. Breaking away from normal routines. As such no planning. No goals, no deadlines. Just work out each day of the next twelve months as he went.

It was a journey that took him through 23 countries, sleeping in 123 different places, visiting amazing destinations and meeting a diverse range of interesting people along the way. Being confronted with issues like drugs, waste, terrorism that have changed his views. How he left with no purpose, other than to travel and explore. But then how a discovery in the middle of a desert created an opportunity that has since benefited charities around the world.

He returned from his journey with one question. Our young generation are travelling the globe in their thousands. Confident and adventurous experience seeking travellers engaging first hand with other cultures. Why is our generation missing out on all the fun? His mission is to change this. To inspire more people, particularly his age, to have the confidence to enjoy adventurous and culturally immersive travel experiences.

www.ingramcontent.com/pod-product-compliance
Lightning Source LLC
Chambersburg PA
CBHW070252010526
44107CB00056B/2437